Kaffe Fassett's
QUILTS in the COTSWOLDS

Medallion quilt designs with Kaffe Collective fabrics

featuring

Liza Prior Lucy
Judy Baldwin
Corienne Kramer
Brandon Mably

The Taunton Press

First published in the USA in 2019 by

The Taunton Press
Inspiration for hands-on living®

The Taunton Press, Inc.,
63 South Main Street,
Newtown, CT 06470
email: tp@taunton.com

Patchwork designs	Kaffe Fassett, Liza Prior Lucy, Judy Baldwin, Corienne Kramer, Brandon Mably
Quilt making coordination	Heart Space Studios (Janet Haigh, Julie Harvey, Ilaria Padovani)
Technical editor	Lin Clements
Quilting	Judy Irish and Mary-Jane Hutchinson
Designer	Anne Wilson
Art direction/styling	Kaffe Fassett
Location photography	Debbie Patterson
Stills photography	Steven Wooster
Illustrations	Heart Space Studios
Publishing consultant	Susan Berry (Berry & Co)

Library of Congress Cataloging-in-Publication Data
in progress

ISBN 978-1-64155-084-0

Colour reproduction	XY Digital, London

Printed in China

Page 1: My *Folded Ribbons* quilt found found its perfect
match on these beautifully weathered boards.
Right: Brandon's Glamping fabric sings out in this lively
little quilt.

Contents

Introduction   4

Dark Gameboard   8, 46

Flowery Jar   10, 86

Malachite Jupiter   12, 50

Russian Knot Garden   14, 59

Golden Medallion   16, 118

Berry Ice Cream   18, 123

Cool Imari Plate   20, 111

Autumn Chintz   22, 77

Jewel Hexagons   24, 100

Graphite Medallion   26, 96

Folded Ribbons   28, 106

Pink Squares   30, 54

Glamping Medallion   32, 64

Sunny Zig Zag   34, 68

Blue Square Dance   36, 72

Sunny Beyond the Border   38, 82

Lavender Ice Cream   40, 128

Chartreuse Basket   42, 132

Autumn Checkerboard   44, 91

Templates   138

Patchwork know-how   146

Glossary of terms   150

Information   151

Distributors and stockists   152

introduction

When I first started taking an interest in patchworks, it was medallion quilts that held a special fascination for me. The idea of a centre panel framed by borders of scrappy piecing was closer to the painting world I inhabited at the time.

This book is really another homage to the long, rich history of the folk art of quilts. Many of the layouts were originally inspired by old recipes found in vintage quilt books but a few I've invented for myself, influenced, as always, by the hours I spend gazing at old quilts, blown away by the endless inventiveness of the geometry that those early quilters came up with.

My favourite design in this book is, however, a completely new one: the *Folded Ribbons* quilt on page 28. We had already decided on the classic Hidcote Gardens as a setting for our book when I designed it. The handsome rustic barn with its weathered boards (where we photographed it) was the starting point for the grey-based colouring I employed in the quilt.

I picked Hidcote for the location for the photography because it was the first British garden to open my eyes to the English genius for creating great theatrical gardens. It is full of surprises with its 'rooms' of different moods and colourings, and its great dramatic spaces framed by stunning yew hedges. To have the insight to create something so deliciously structured, coupled with the amazing patience to sit by year after year until it matures into being,

is phenomenal, particularly to a crazed result seeker like me!

Hidcote was started in the early 1900s near Stratford upon Avon by Major Lawrence Johnston, an American by birth who became a naturalized British subject in 1900, and who became a plant hunter of repute. As an American myself who has made England my home, I can well imagine Johnston's love of English gardens as he grew his amazing vision. How wonderful that Hidcote, tucked away in the rural Cotswolds of England, continues to be lovingly groomed by the National Trust for all of us in need of a spiritual lift, to visit and receive benediction. I hope in this humble book you get enough of an impression of my favourite English garden to pay it a visit and see, using all your senses, how totally enchanting the whole effect is.

There wasn't a quilt made by my team that didn't find a perfect setting in the garden's many moods. We split the photography for this book into two shoots – one in June to catch the spring and summer colourings and another in September for those rich autumn tones.

It's always very exciting each year to use our new prints in various colour combinations, but I particularly love reworking a previous layout in a fresh colour scheme with the latest Kaffe Fassett Collective designs that we produce each year.

Dark Gameboard
by Kaffe Fassett

I used all our deepest prints for my dark version of Liza Prior Lucy's original quilt. It settles gorgeously into Hidcote's impressively sculpted yew hedges. The topiary here is so distinctive, creating one of the magic 'rooms' in the garden.

Flowery Jar
by Kaffe Fassett

When I picked the prints for this version of *Flowery Jar*, it was with the English early summer blooms at Hidcote in mind. I was delighted to find how well it fitted into this deliciously pastel border with its classic flowers in soft pinks, blues and mauves.

Malachite Jupiter
by Kaffe Fassett

This little jewel of a pergola at Hidcote creates a pleasing change of pace. Its delightful murals and collections of leafy plants created a shady setting for my recolouring of Julie Stockler's original small *Jupiter* quilt. I couldn't resist stopping for a rest under the ferns. (In fact, I look like I have been painted into the mural behind me!)

Russian Knot Garden
by Kaffe Fassett

This bank of purple loosestrife (*Lythrum salicaria*) echoes the rich palette of the *Knot Garden* quilt.

Golden Medallion
by Liza Prior Lucy

A small shed in a corner of the garden became the perfect setting for this glowing amber-toned quilt. The dusty wooden surfaces and blond tones of the hanging bunches of dried flowers make the quilt radiate warmth.

Berry Ice Cream
by Kaffe Fassett

This is a layout I love to play with and is about the fourth version I have done. The colours were inspired by the famous Red Border at Hidcote, which acts here as its backdrop. For a delicious pastel version, look at *Lavender Ice Cream* on page 40.

Cool Imari Plate
by Corienne Kramer

Corienne's cool palette for her recoloured version of my Imari Plate quilt looked just right on this classical garden gate. It stands at the start of an impressively tall avenue of trees that you pass through on the way to the gardens.

Autumn Chintz
by Kaffe Fassett

The golden stone of Hidcote's entrance building stopped us in our tracks. Doesn't our *Autumn Chintz* glow in this setting?

OVERLEAF

Jewel Hexagons
by Liza Prior Lucy

How alive the colours of this aptly named quilt become when brought to this jewel-like setting! The stone columns and ironwork make a romantic structure to contain the lush abundance of flowers, like the bellflowers (*Campanula latiloba*), climbing sweet pea (*Lathyrus grandiflora*), *Philadelphus*, old-fashioned pink roses and geraniums.

Graphite Medallion
by Kaffe Fassett

This delightful rustic-inspired bench and the dark yew hedge behind make the ideal setting for this cool-toned variation of a favourite Checkerboard design. *Autumn Checkerboard*, a warmer-coloured version by Liza Prior Lucy, can be seen on page 45.

Folded Ribbons
by Kaffe Fassett

This is the one quilt in this book for which I did a new design and my colouring for it had this barn in mind. The sculptured wooden cladding, thick beams and thatched roof made the architecture stick in my head when I was designing this quilt.

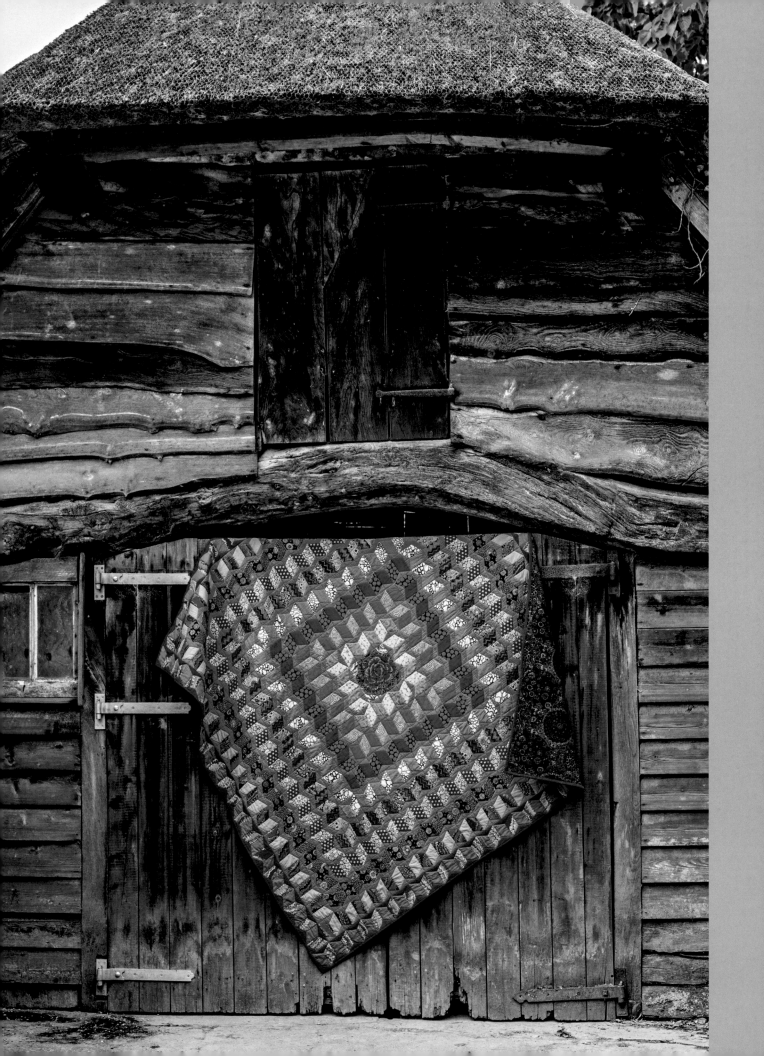

Pink Squares
by Kaffe Fassett

I used a classic vintage quilt as a starting point for this layout. The vivid pink sashing and high pastels of the fussy-cut floral prints make it sing, echoing the flowers and foliage at Hidcote, some of which are featured here. Clockwise, from top left: perennial sweet pea (*Lathyrus grandiflora*), *Eryngium* 'Miss Willmott's Ghost', *Dahlia* 'Betty Anne', *Helianthemum* 'Lemon Queen', *Rosa* 'Frencham', cabbages and kale, *Cosmos* 'Picotee' and *Kniphofia* 'Tawny King'.

Glamping Medallion
by Kaffe Fassett

Brandon's Glamping print,
with its jaunty striped tents,
is perfect on this classic
garden pergola at Hidcote.
The doorway frames one
of the grandest avenues in
the gardens.

Sunny Zig Zag
by Kaffe Fassett

This handsome giant Datura plant, along with the lively yellow daisies, caught my eye, leading me to choose this corner to show off the honey tones of this medallion quilt.

Blue Square Dance
by Kaffe Fassett

When I'm designing ranges, I always try to provide people with a classic blue and white print or two – it's a combination that never dates as can be seen in my version of Julie Stockler's original quilt. The slates and weathered barn contrast so elegantly here.

Sunny beyond the Border
by Brandon Mably

Brandon's recolouring of this quilt uses mostly his new prints with some of mine. It really glows against the Cotswold stone of the building and the autumnal foliage in this corner of the garden.

Lavender Ice Cream
by Kaffe Fassett

The deep lavender tiles in the little garden pergola at Hidcote were absolutely right to show off the glowing pastels of this re-envisioned quilt. For a colourway inspired by Hidcote's Red Border see *Berry Ice Cream* on page 19.

40

Chartreuse Basket
by Judy Baldwin

All the shades of lime and high greeny yellows in this corner of the garden really make Judy's version of Betsy Mennesson's original quilt sing. My shirt was an appropriate choice as well! The new Sunburst print (below left) makes the perfect backing for this quilt.

43

Autumn Checkerboard
by Liza Prior Lucy

What setting could be better to show off the rich palette of this quilt than this mossy roof and the bronzy tones of a smoke bush? For a cool-toned version see *Graphite Medallion* on page 27.

dark gameboard **

Kaffe Fassett

This dramatic quilt has a fussy-cut centre square, which is surrounded by a series of pieced triangular sections, added in 'rounds' to create an on-point layout. Four different sizes of squares are used, with four different sizes of triangles – all easily cut from width-of-fabric strips.

SIZE OF FINISHED QUILT
90in x 90in (228.5cm x 228.5cm)

FABRICS
Fabrics calculated at minimum width of 40in (102cm) and are cut across the width, unless otherwise stated. Fabrics have been given a number – see Fabric Swatch Diagram for details.

Patchwork Fabrics
LOTUS LEAF
| Fabric 1 | Dark | 1yd (90cm) |

JAPANESE CHRYSANTHEMUM
| Fabric 2 | Antique | 2yd (1.8m) |

ABORIGINAL DOT
Fabric 3	Orchid	1¼yd (1.2m)
Fabric 4	Chocolate	¾yd (70cm)
Fabric 5	Charcoal	⅜yd (40cm)

MAD PLAID
| Fabric 6 | Purple | 1¼yd (1.2m) |

SPOT
| Fabric 7 | Black | 1⅛yd (1m) |
| Fabric 8 | Bottle | ½yd (45cm) |

MOSS
| Fabric 9 | Black | ½yd (45cm) |

Backing and Binding Fabrics
MOSS
| Fabric 9 | Black | 7yd (6.4m) |

SPOT
| Fabric 7 | Black | ¾yd (70cm) |

Batting
98in x 98in (249cm x 249cm)

PATCHES
The patch shapes needed have each been given a letter to identify them in the instructions. All patches were cut from strips across the width of the fabric and then sub-cut into squares and right-angled triangles in the following sizes:
Square A: 3⅛in (8cm).
Square B: 4¼in (10.8cm).
Square C: 5⅞in (15cm).
Square D: 8in (20.3cm).
The triangle patches are created from squares, cut in half along one diagonal.
Triangle E: 3½in (9cm).
Triangle F: 4⅝in (11.7cm).
Triangle G: 6¼in (15.9cm).
Triangle H: 8⅜in (21.3cm).

The quilt centre is a fussy-cut square 23in (58.4cm). The is square is then surrounded with a series of pieced triangular sections ('rounds'). See Diagram 2 on page 49 for the quilt layout.

The first round (closest to centre square) is pieced using Square A and Triangle E.
The second round is pieced using Square B and Triangle F.
The third round is pieced using Square C and Triangle G.
The fourth round is pieced using Square D and Triangle H.

CUTTING OUT
Cut the fabric in the order stated. We have listed the cutting for the rounds of pieced triangles and the centre square separately, working from the outside inwards, i.e. largest (outermost Round 4) to smallest (innermost Round 1) to prevent waste.

Centre square
From Fabric 1 choose your favourite motifs and fussy cut a 23in (58.4cm) square.

FABRIC SWATCH DIAGRAM

Patchwork Fabrics

 Fabric 1
LOTUS LEAF
Dark
GP29DK

 Fabric 2
JAPANESE
CHRYSANTHEMUM
Antique
PJ41AN

 Fabric 3
ABORIGINAL DOT
Orchid
GP71OD

 Fabric 4
ABORIGINAL DOT
Chocolate
GP71CL

 Fabric 5
ABORIGINAL DOT
Charcoal
GP71CC

 Fabric 6
MAD PLAID
Purple
BM37PU

 Fabric 7
SPOT
Black
GP70BK

 Fabric 8
SPOT
Bottle
GP70BT

 Fabric 9
MOSS
Black
BM68BK

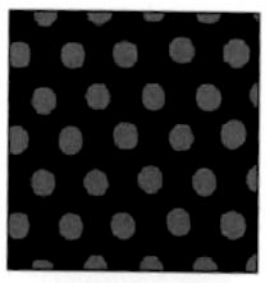

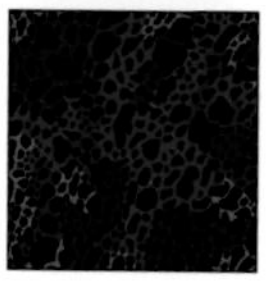

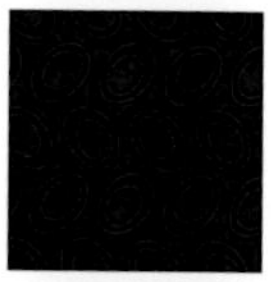

Backing and Binding Fabrics

 Fabric 9
MOSS
Black
BM68BK

 Fabric 7
SPOT
Black
GP70BK

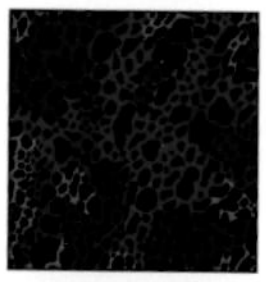

Round 4

From Fabric 2 cut 8in (20.3cm) strips across the width of the fabric. Each strip will give 5 of Square D. Cut 24 squares in total.

From Fabric 3 cut 8in (20.3cm) strips across the width of the fabric. Each strip will give 5 of Square D. Cut 36 squares in total.

From Fabric 2 cut 8³⁄₈in (21.3cm) strips across the width of the fabric. Each strip will give 4 squares. Sub-cut into 8 of Triangle H. Cut 24 triangles in total.

Round 3

From Fabric 6 cut 5⁷⁄₈in (15cm) strips across the width of the fabric. Each strip will give 6 of Square C. Cut 24 squares in total.

From Fabric 7 cut 5⁷⁄₈in (15cm) strips across the width of the fabric. Each strip will give 6 of Square C. Cut 36 squares in total.

From Fabric 6 cut 6¼in (15.9cm) strips across the width of the fabric. Each strip will give 6 squares. Sub-cut into 12 of Triangle G. Cut 24 triangles in total.

Round 2

From Fabric 4 cut 4¼in (10.8cm) strips across the width of the fabric. Each strip will give 9 of Square B. Cut 24 squares in total.

From Fabric 8 cut 4¼in (10.8cm) strips across the width of the fabric. Each strip will give 9 of Square B. Cut 36 squares in total.

From Fabric 4 cut 4⁵⁄₈in (11.7cm) strips across the width of the fabric. Each strip will give 8 squares. Sub-cut into 16 of Triangle F. Cut 24 triangles in total.

Round 1

From Fabric 9 cut 3¹⁄₈in (8cm) strips across the width of the fabric. Each strip will give 12 of Square A. Cut 24 squares in total.

From Fabric 5 cut 3¹⁄₈in (8cm) strips across the width of the fabric. Each strip will give 12 of Square A. Cut 36 squares in total.

From Fabric 9 cut 3½in (9cm) strips across the width of the fabric. Each strip will give 11 squares. Sub-cut into 22 of Triangle E. Cut 24 triangles in total.

DIAGRAM 1

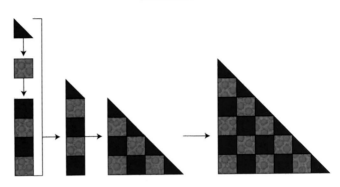

Backing

From backing Fabric 9 cut 2 pieces 40in x 98in (102cm x 249cm) and 2 pieces 19½in x 50in (49.5cm x 127cm).

Binding

From binding Fabric 7 cut 10 strips 2½in (6.4cm) wide across the width of the fabric. Sew together end to end.

MAKING THE QUILT

Use a ¼in (6mm) seam allowance throughout. The triangular sections in each round are made in the same way, using the appropriate sizes of squares and triangles – follow Diagram 1 for the piecing sequence. Each round will need four triangular sections.

Once the four triangular sections for Round 1 are made, sew two sections to opposite sides of the centre square. Press and then add the other two sections to the remaining sides.

Piece Round 2, Round 3 and Round 4 in the same way, and add them to the quilt in the same manner, easing to fit as necessary.

FINISHING THE QUILT

Press the quilt top. Using a ¼in (6mm) seam allowance, sew the 2 backing pieces 19½in x 50in (49.5cm x 127cm) together into one long strip. Sew this between the other two larger pieces of backing to form a piece approx. 98in x 98in (249cm x 249cm).

Layer the quilt top, batting and backing and baste together (see page 148). Quilt as desired.

Trim the quilt edges and attach the binding (see page 149).

DIAGRAM 2

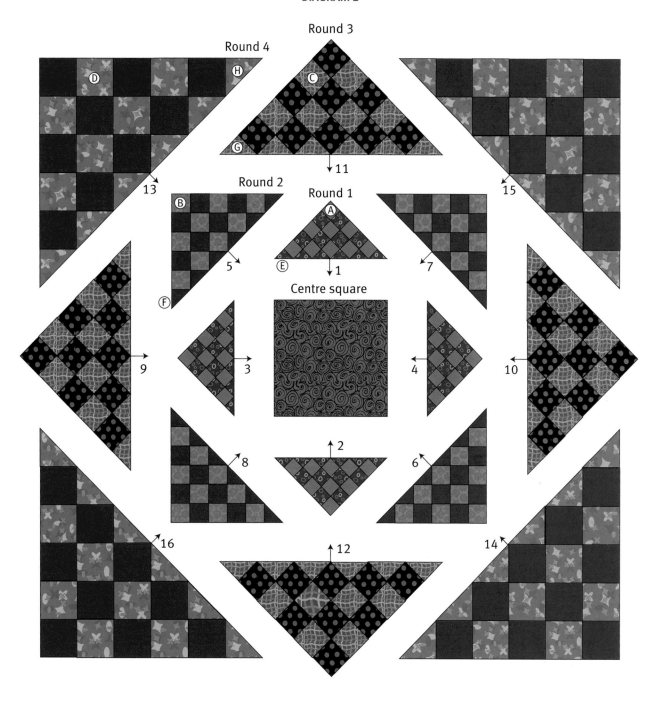

Round 3

Round 4

Round 2

Round 1

C

H

D

G

11

B

A

5

E

1

F

Centre square

9

3

4

10

8

2

6

16

12

14

13

15

7

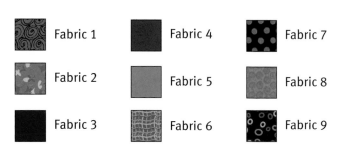

	Fabric 1		Fabric 4		Fabric 7
	Fabric 2		Fabric 5		Fabric 8
	Fabric 3		Fabric 6		Fabric 9

49

malachite jupiter **

Kaffe Fassett

This medallion quilt, in wonderful rich greens, is made more interesting by having its inner borders arranged on point and its outer border squares also on point, filled in with triangles.

SIZE OF FINISHED QUILT
42½in x 42½in (108cm x 108cm)

FABRICS
Fabrics calculated at minimum width of 40in (102cm) and are cut across the width, unless otherwise stated. Fabrics have been given a number – see Fabric Swatch Diagram for details.

Patchwork Fabrics

POPPY GARDEN		
Fabric 1	Green	¾yd (70cm)
JUPITER		
Fabric 2	Malachite	¼yd (25cm)
SUCCULENT		
Fabric 3	Pink	¼yd (25cm)
ZIG ZAG		
Fabric 4	Moody	⅛yd (15cm)
LACY LEAF		
Fabric 5	Green	⅜yd (40cm)
ROMAN GLASS		
Fabric 6	Emerald	¼yd (25cm)
COLEUS		
Fabric 7	Moss	⅜yd (40cm)
END PAPERS		
Fabric 8	Purple	¼yd (25cm)
LADY'S PURSE		
Fabric 9	Antique	¼yd (25cm)
SPOT		
Fabric 10	Green	½yd (45cm)
ORCHID		
Fabric 11	Blue	Use spare backing fabric

Backing and Binding Fabrics

ORCHID		
Fabric 11	Blue	2⅞ yd (2.65m)
SPOT		
Fabric 12	Sapphire	½yd (45cm)

Batting
50in x 50in (127cm x 127cm)

TEMPLATE

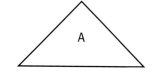

FABRIC SWATCH DIAGRAM

Patchwork Fabrics

Fabric 1
POPPY GARDEN
Green
PJ95GN

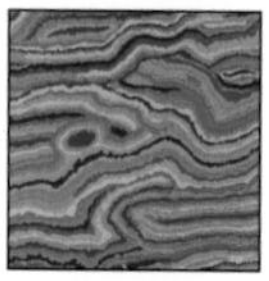

Fabric 2
JUPITER
Malachite
GP131MA

Fabric 3
SUCCULENT
Pink
PJ91PK

Fabric 4
ZIG ZAG
Moody
BM43MO

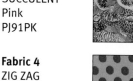

Fabric 5
LACY LEAF
Green
PJ93GN

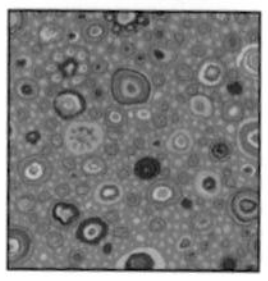

Fabric 6
ROMAN GLASS
Emerald
GP01EM

Fabric 7
COLEUS
Moss
PJ30MS

Fabric 8
END PAPERS
Purple
GP159PU

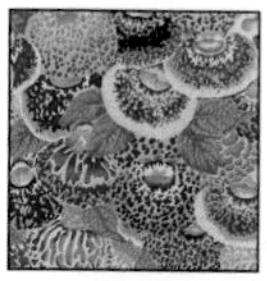

Fabric 9
LADY'S PURSE
Antique
PJ94AN

Fabric 10
SPOT
Green
GP70GN

Fabric 11
ORCHID
Blue
PJ92BL

Backing and Binding Fabrics

Fabric 11
ORCHID
Blue
PJ92BL

Fabric 12
SPOT
Sapphire
GP70SP

CUTTING OUT
Quilt Centre
From Fabric 1 fussy cut a square 10in (25.4cm).
From Fabric 2 cut 2 squares 7⅝in (19.4cm). Cut each square in half once along the diagonal to make 4 triangles.

Border 1
From Fabric 3 cut 4 strips 3¼in x 14in (8.3cm x 35.5cm).
From Fabric 4 cut 4 squares 3¼in (8.3cm) for corner squares.

Border 2
From Fabric 5 and using Template A, cut 12 triangles, with the straight grain of the fabric running along the long side of the triangle. Rotate the template 180 degrees alternately for best use of the fabric.
From Fabric 6 and using Template A, cut 16 triangles, as before.

From Fabric 7 cut 2 squares 10⅞in (27.6cm). Cut each square in half once diagonally to make 4 triangles.

Border 3
From Fabric 1 cut 4 strips 4⅛in x 27¼in (10.5cm x 69.2cm).
From Fabric 8 cut 4 squares 4⅛in (10.5cm) for corner squares.

Border 4
From Fabric 5 cut 16 squares 3½in (9cm).
From Fabric 9 cut 16 squares 3½in (9cm).
From Fabric 10 cut three 5½in (14cm) strips across the width of the fabric. Cut each strip into 5½in (14cm) squares and then cut each square twice diagonally into 4 triangles (this is so the long side of the triangles do not have a bias edge). Cut 72 triangles in total.
From Fabric 11 fussy cut 4 squares 4¾in (12cm) for corner squares.
Note: cut the backing fabric pieces before you fussy cut these squares.

DIAGRAM 1

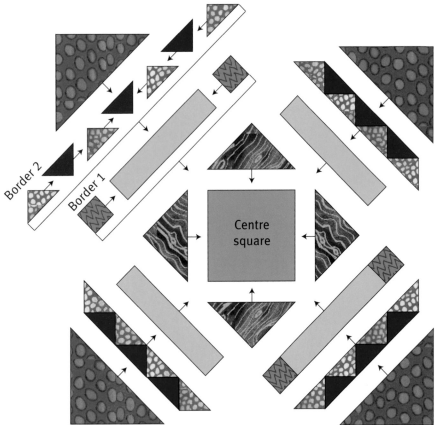

Border 2

Border 1

Centre
square

Backing
From backing Fabric 11 cut a piece
40in x 50in (102cm x 127cm) and a piece
11in x 50in (28cm x 127cm). Reserve the
spare for the Border 4 corner squares.

Binding
From Fabric 12 cut 5 strips 2½in (6.4cm)
wide across the width of the fabric. Sew
together end to end.

MAKING THE QUILT
Use a ¼in (6mm) seam allowance
throughout and refer to Diagram 1
and Diagram 2 for assembly and fabric
placement.

Quilt centre Take the centre square and
sew a Fabric 2 7⅝in (19.4cm) triangle
to opposite sides. Add the other 2
triangles on the other sides, as shown in
Diagram 1.

Border 1 Sew two border strips to the
sides of the quilt. Add the Fabric 4 corner
squares to the ends of the other 2 strips
and sew these to the quilt.

DIAGRAM 2

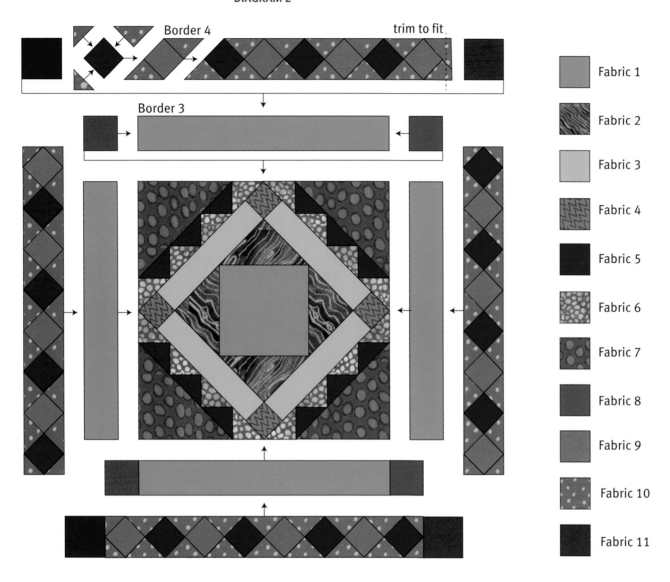

Fabric 1
Fabric 2
Fabric 3
Fabric 4
Fabric 5
Fabric 6
Fabric 7
Fabric 8
Fabric 9
Fabric 10
Fabric 11

Border 2 Piece the triangle sections using the Template A triangles, alternating the fabrics (see Diagram 1). Sew the pieced strips to the sides of the quilt. Add the $10^7/_8$ in (27.6cm) triangles from Fabric 7.

Border 3 Sew two border strips to the sides of the quilt. Add the corner squares to the ends of the other 2 strips and sew these to the quilt (see Diagram 2).

Border 4 Piece a border section by sewing a triangle to each side of a $3^1/_2$ in (9cm) square, as in Diagram 2. Repeat to make 4 border strips. Trim the length, as

needed, to match the quilt exactly and add 2 strips to the sides of the quilt. Trim the other 2 strips to length and then add the Fabric 11 corner squares to the ends of the 2 strips and sew to the quilt.

FINISHING THE QUILT
Press the quilt top. Sew the backing pieces together using a $^1/_4$ in (6mm) seam allowance to form a piece approx. 50in (127cm) square.
Layer the quilt top, batting and backing and baste together (see page 148).
Quilt as desired.
Trim the quilt edges and attach the binding (see page 149).

pink squares **

Kaffe Fassett

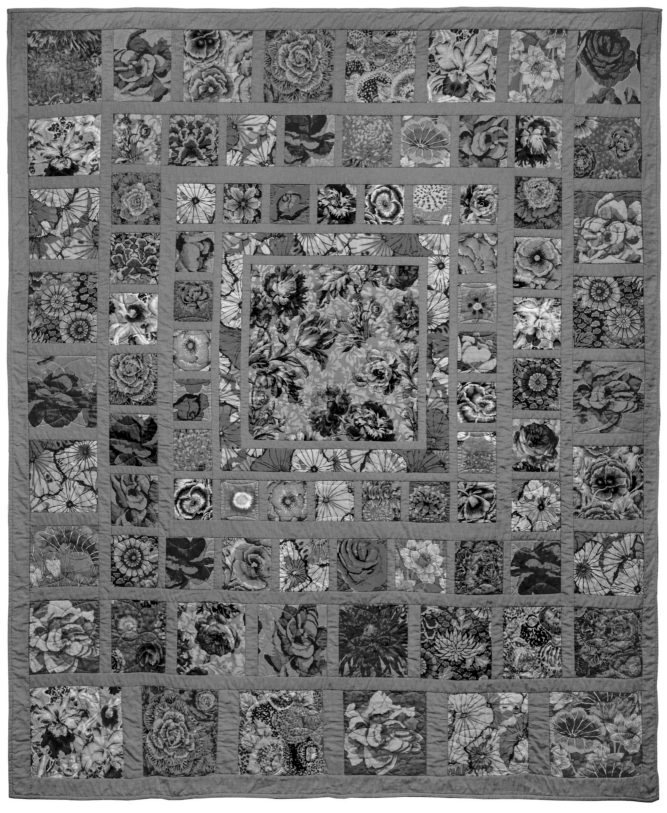

This quilt has eight borders around a central panel. The unpieced borders are alternated with pieced borders, which use different sized squares separated by sashing strips. An extra pieced and unpieced border at the bottom of the quilt creates an interesting off-centre look. Fabric quantities are generous to allow enough for fussy cutting the flower motifs.

FABRIC SWATCH DIAGRAM

Patchwork Fabrics

Fabric 1
BAROQUE FLORAL
Red
PJ90RD

Fabric 2
LOTUS LEAF
Citrus
GP29CT

Fabric 3
LOTUS LEAF
Lime
GP29LM

Fabric 4
POPPY GARDEN
Red
PJ95RD

Fabric 5
POPPY GARDEN
Pink
PJ95PK

Fabric 6
ROSE CLOUDS
Magenta
GP164MG

Fabric 7
ROSE CLOUDS
Aqua
GP164AQ

Fabric 8
ORCHID
Natural
PJ92NL

Fabric 9
BRASSICA
Red
PJ21RD

Fabric 10
DREAM
Red
GP148RD

Fabric 11
BIG BLOOMS
Turquoise
GP91TQ

Fabric 12
BIG BLOOMS
Green
GP91GN

Fabric 13
JAPANESE CHRYSANTHEMUM
Pink
PJ41PK

Fabric 14
LAKE BLOSSOM
Magenta
GP93MG

Fabric 15
LADY'S PURSE
Ochre
PJ94OC

Fabric 16
ABORIGINAL DOT
Shocking
GP71SG

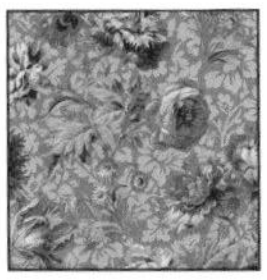

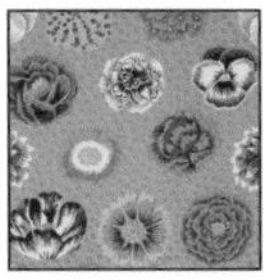

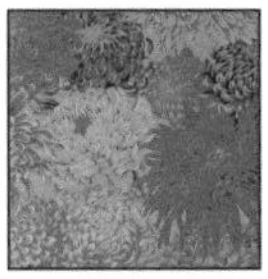

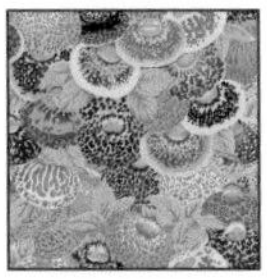

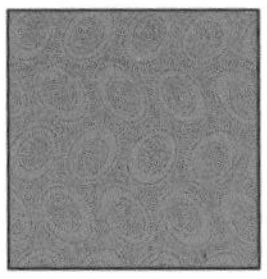

Backing and Binding Fabrics

Fabric 17
CARPET
Red
QBGP001RD

Fabric 16
ABORIGINAL DOT
Shocking
GP71SG

SIZE OF FINISHED QUILT
76in x 87in (193cm x 221cm)

FABRICS
Fabrics calculated at minimum width of 40in (102cm) and are cut across the width, unless otherwise stated. Fabrics have been given a number – see Fabric Swatch Diagram for details.

Patchwork Fabrics

BAROQUE FLORAL		
Fabric 1	Red	½yd (45cm)
LOTUS LEAF		
Fabric 2	Citrus	¾yd (70cm)
Fabric 3	Lime	½yd (45cm)
POPPY GARDEN		
Fabric 4	Red	½yd (45cm)
Fabric 5	Pink	¼yd (25cm)
ROSE CLOUDS		
Fabric 6	Magenta	½yd (45cm)
Fabric 7	Aqua	¾yd (70cm)
ORCHID		
Fabric 8	Natural	½yd (45cm)
BRASSICA		
Fabric 9	Red	½yd (45cm)
DREAM		
Fabric 10	Red	⅝yd (60cm)
BIG BLOOMS		
Fabric 11	Turquoise	⅜yd (40cm)
Fabric 12	Green	¼yd (25cm)
JAPANESE CHRYSANTHEMUM		
Fabric 13	Pink	⅜yd (40cm)
LAKE BLOSSOM		
Fabric 14	Magenta	½yd (45cm)
LADY'S PURSE		
Fabric 15	Ochre	½yd (45cm)
ABORIGINAL DOT		
Fabric 16	Shocking	2¾yd (2.5m)

Backing and Binding Fabrics

CARPET		
Fabric 17	Red	2½yd (2.3m)

of extra-wide fabric (108in/274cm)

ABORIGINAL DOT		
Fabric 16	Shocking	¾yd (70cm)

Batting
84in x 95in (213.4cm x 241.3cm)

PATCHES

Refer to Diagram 1 (see page 57) and Diagram 2 (see page 58) for the quilt layout. The quilt is made up of various square and rectangular patches cut from Fabrics 1 to 15. These are joined by sashing rectangles of Fabric 16. The various patches are referred to by a capital letter in the instructions, and the cut sizes are as follows:

Centre square: 20in (50.8cm).
Square A for Border 4: 5in (12.7cm).
Square B for Border 6: 6¼in (16cm).
Square C for Border 8: 8½in (21.6cm).
Rectangle D for Border 8: 8½in x 7¼in (21.6cm x 18.4cm).
Square E for Bottom Row: 10in (25.4cm).
Rectangle F for Bottom Row: 11¼in x 10in (28.6cm x 25.4cm).

CUTTING OUT

Centre Square
From Fabric 1 cut a square 20in (50.8cm).

Floral Squares and Rectangles
Fussy cut all of these shapes:
From Fabric 1 cut 2 x A, 3 x B and 1 x C.
From Fabric 2 cut 1 x A, 1 x B, 2 x C and 1 x D.
From Fabric 3 cut 1 x A, 2 x B and 1 x E.
From Fabric 4 cut 4 x A, 2 x B and 2 x C.
From Fabric 5 cut 3 x A.
From Fabric 6 cut 2 x A, 2 x B, 2 x C and 1 x E.
From Fabric 7 cut 2 x A, 5 x B, 4 x C and 1 x D.
From Fabric 8 cut 2 x B, 1 x C, 1 x D and 1 x F.
From Fabric 9 cut 3 x B, 2 x C and 1 x E.
From Fabric 10 cut 1 x A, 4 x B and 3 x C.
From Fabric 11 cut 2 x A and 2 x D.
From Fabric 12 cut 4 x A.
From Fabric 13 cut 2 x A, 2 x B and 2 x C.
From Fabric 14 cut 2 x B, 2 x D and 1 x F.
From Fabric 15 cut 1 x C, 1 x D and 1 x E.
In total you should have: 24 x Square A, 28 x Square B, 20 x Square C, 8 x Rectangle D, 4 x Square E and 2 x Rectangle F.

Unpieced Borders and Sashing
Border 1 From Fabric 16 cut 3 strips 1½in (3.8cm) wide across the width of the fabric, join as necessary and cut 2 borders 1½in x 20in (3.8cm x 50.8cm) for the quilt top and bottom and 2 borders 1½in x 22in (3.8cm x 56cm) for the quilt sides.

Border 2 From Fabric 2 cut 3 strips 3in (7.6cm) wide across the width of the fabric, join as necessary and cut 2 borders 3in x 22in (7.6cm x 56cm) for the quilt top and bottom and 2 borders 3in x 27in (7.6cm x 68.6cm) for the quilt sides.

Border 3 From Fabric 16 cut 3 strips 1½in (3.8cm) wide across the width of the fabric, join as necessary and cut 2 borders 1½in x 27in (3.8cm x 68.6cm) for the quilt top and bottom and 2 borders 1½in x 29in (3.8cm x 73.7cm) for the quilt sides.

Border 4 Sashing Strips From Fabric 16 cut 3 strips 1½in (3.8cm) wide across the width of the fabric, then cut 24 sashing strips 1½in x 5in (3.8cm x 12.7cm).

Border 5 From Fabric 16 cut 5 strips 2½in (6.4cm) wide across the width of the fabric, join as necessary and cut 2 borders 2½in x 38in (6.4cm x 96.5cm) for the quilt top and bottom and 2 borders 2½in x 42in (6.4cm x 106.7cm) for the quilt sides.

Border 6 Sashing Strips From Fabric 16 cut 5 strips 1½in (3.8cm) wide across the width of the fabric, then cut 28 strips 1½in x 6¼in (3.8cm x 15.9cm).

Border 7 From Fabric 16 cut 6 strips 2in (5.1cm) wide across the width of the fabric, join as necessary and cut 2 borders 2in x 53½in (5.1cm x 135.9cm) for the quilt top and bottom and 2 borders 2in x 56½in (5.1cm x 143.5cm) for the quilt sides.

Border 8 Sashing Strips From Fabric 16 cut 7 strips 2in (5.1cm) wide across the width of the fabric, then cut 28 strips 2in x 8½in (5.1cm x 21.6cm).

Bottom Sashing Strip From Fabric 16 cut 2 strips 2in (5.1cm) wide across the width of the fabric, join as necessary and cut a strip 2in x 72½in (5.1cm x 184.2cm).

Bottom Row Sashing Strips From Fabric 16 cut 2 strips 3in (7.6cm) wide across the width of the fabric, then cut 5 sashing strips 3in x 10in (7.6cm x 25.4cm).

Outer Border From Fabric 16 cut 9 strips 2½in (6.4cm) wide across the width of the fabric, join as necessary and cut 2 strips

2½in x 72½in (6.4cm x 184.2cm) for the quilt top and bottom and 2 strips 2½in x 87½in (6.4cm x 222.2cm).

Backing
From backing Fabric 17 cut a piece 84in x 95in (213.4cm x 241.3cm).

Binding
From Fabric 16 cut 9 strips 2½in (6.4cm) wide across the width of the fabric. Sew together end to end.

MAKING THE QUILT
Use a ¼in (6mm) seam allowance throughout. Refer to Diagram 1 and Diagram 2 on page 58 for layout and fabric placement. Take care to add the borders in the numbered order shown in the diagrams.

Borders 1–3 To the centre square add the Border 1 strips, top and bottom first, and then the sides.
Add the Border 2 strips and then the Border 3 strips in the same sequence, as in Diagram 1.

Border 4 Border 4 is pieced using 24 A squares interspaced with sashing strips. Piece the top and bottom border, each with 5 A squares and 6 sashing strips. Sew to the quilt. Piece the side borders, each with 7 A squares and 6 sashing strips. Sew to the quilt sides.

Border 5 Add the Border 5 strips, top and bottom first, and then the sides.

Borders 6–8 Border 6 is pieced using 28 B squares interspaced with sashing strips. Piece the top and bottom border, each of 6 B squares and 7 sashing strips. Sew to the quilt. Piece the side borders, each with 8 B squares and 7 sashing strips. Sew to the quilt sides, as shown in Diagram 2 on page 58.
Add the Border 7 strips, top and bottom first, and then the sides.
Border 8 is pieced using 20 C squares and 8 D rectangles interspaced with sashing strips. Refer to Diagram 2 for the layout of these shapes. Piece the top and bottom borders as shown and add to the quilt top and bottom. Piece the sides and add to the quilt sides.
Now add only the top outer border and then the bottom sashing strip.

Bottom Row This row is pieced using 4 E squares, 2 F rectangles and the bottom row sashing strips. Refer to Diagram 2 for the layout of these shapes and piece as shown.

Outer Border Add the bottom outer border to the quilt bottom and then the side outer borders to complete the quilt.

FINISHING THE QUILT
Press the quilt top.
Layer the quilt top, batting and backing and baste together (see page 148).
Quilt as desired.
Trim the quilt edges and attach the binding (see page 149).

DIAGRAM 1

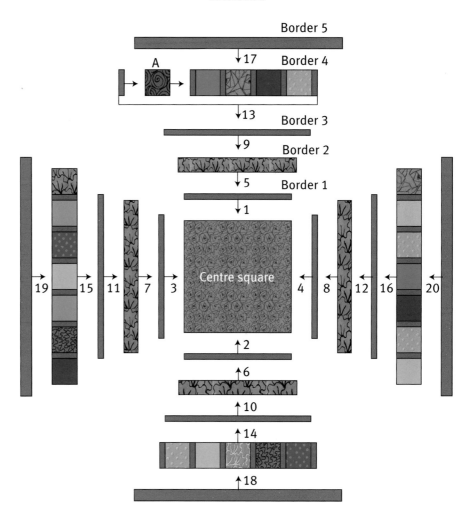

DIAGRAM 2

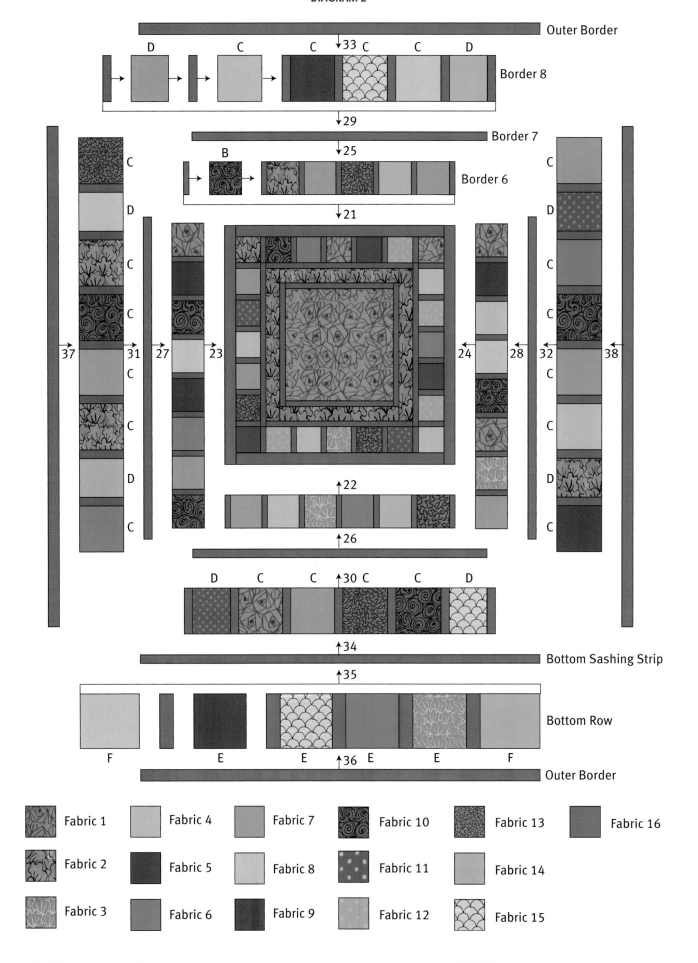

Outer Border

Border 8

D C C 33 C C D

29

Border 7

25

B

Border 6

21

37 31 27 23 24 28 32 38

C D C C C C D C

22

26

D C C 30 C C D

34

Bottom Sashing Strip

35

Bottom Row

F E E 36 E E F

Outer Border

Fabric 1	Fabric 4	Fabric 7	Fabric 10	Fabric 13	Fabric 16
Fabric 2	Fabric 5	Fabric 8	Fabric 11	Fabric 14	
Fabric 3	Fabric 6	Fabric 9	Fabric 12	Fabric 15	

russian knot garden ***

Kaffe Fassett

This striking medallion-style quilt is challenging but well worth the effort. A fussy-cut centre square is surrounded by seven borders in total.

SIZE OF FINISHED QUILT
73in x 73in (185.5cm x 185.5cm)

FABRICS
Fabrics calculated at minimum width of 40in (102cm) and are cut across the width, unless otherwise stated. Fabrics have been given a number – see Fabric Swatch Diagram for details.

Patchwork Fabrics

ENCHANTED
| Fabric 1 | Red | ³⁄₈yd (40cm) |
| Fabric 2 | Dark | 1¹⁄₈yd (1m) |

MAD PLAID
| Fabric 3 | Maroon | ³⁄₈yd (40cm) |

DIAMOND STRIPE
| Fabric 4 | Red | ¹⁄₂yd (45cm) |

JUMBLE
| Fabric 5 | Rust | ¹⁄₄yd (25cm) |
| Fabric 6 | Blue | 1¹⁄₄yd (1.2m) |

GOOD VIBRATIONS
| Fabric 7 | Orange | ¹⁄₄yd (25cm) |

SPOT
| Fabric 8 | Royal | 1¹⁄₄yd (1.2m) |
| Fabric 9 | Black | ¹⁄₂yd (45cm) |

POMEGRANATE
| Fabric 10 | Black | ¹⁄₄yd (25cm) |

LACY LEAF
| Fabric 11 | Red | ³⁄₄yd (70cm) |

SHARKS TEETH
| Fabric 12 | Rose | ¹⁄₄yd (25cm) |

WHIRLIGIG
| Fabric 13 | Tomato | ¹⁄₄yd (25cm) |

GUINEA FLOWER
| Fabric 14 | Red | ¹⁄₄yd (25cm) |

ROW FLOWERS
| Fabric 15 | Red | ¹⁄₈yd (15cm) |

FEATHERS
| Fabric 16 | Turquoise | ¹⁄₄yd (25cm) |

Backing and Binding Fabrics

CARPET
| Fabric 17 | Black | 2¹⁄₂yd (2.3m) |

of extra-wide fabric (108in/274cm)

MILLEFIORE
| Fabric 18 | Blue | ³⁄₄yd (70cm) |

Batting
81in x 81in (206cm x 206cm)

FABRIC SWATCH DIAGRAM

Patchwork Fabrics

Fabric 1
ENCHANTED
Red
GP172RD

Fabric 2
ENCHANTED
Dark
GP172DK

Fabric 3
MAD PLAID
Maroon
BM37MR

Fabric 4
DIAMOND STRIPE
Red
GP170RD

Fabric 5
JUMBLE
Rust
BM53RU

Fabric 6
JUMBLE
Blue
BM53BL

Fabric 7
GOOD VIBRATIONS
Orange
BM65OR

Fabric 8
SPOT
Royal
GP70RY

Fabric 9
SPOT
Black
GP70BK

Fabric 10
POMEGRANATE
Black
BM67BK

Fabric 11
LACY LEAF
Red
PJ93RD

Fabric 12
SHARKS TEETH
Rose
BM60RO

Fabric 13
WHIRLIGIG
Tomato
GP166TM

Fabric 14
GUINEA FLOWER
Red
GP59RD

Fabric 15
ROW FLOWERS
Red
GP169RD

Fabric 16
FEATHERS
Turquoise
PJ55TQ

Backing and Binding Fabrics

Fabric 17
CARPET
Black
QBGP001BK

Fabric 18
MILLEFIORE
Blue
GP92BL

TEMPLATES

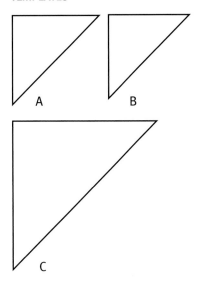

PATCHES

This quilt is formed around a fussy-cut centre square. It has 4 unpieced borders (Borders 1, 3, 5 and 7), alternated with 3 pieced borders (Borders 2, 4 and 6). The quilt has many square and triangle patches – see Diagram 1 and Diagram 2 on page 62 and Diagram 3 on page 63 for identification and the border in which they are used.

Sizes for the squares are given in Cutting Out.

Three of the triangles are right-angled and can be cut from squares.

Triangle a is cut from a 7⅝in (19.4cm) square and is used for the large triangles sewn to the centre square.

Triangle b is cut from a 7⅞in (20cm) square and is used for the large triangles sewn to Border 2.

Triangle c is cut from a 5⅛in (13cm) square and is used for the right-angled triangles in Border 6.

Three triangles need templates (see pages 140 and 141), so that the long edge of the triangle is on the fabric grain.

Template A – used in Border 2.
Template B – used in Border 4.
Template C – used in Border 6.

CUTTING OUT

Centre square

From Fabric 1 fussy cut a 10in (25.4cm) square.

From Fabric 3 cut 2 squares 7⅝in (19.4cm). Cut each square in half once diagonally to make 4 of Triangle a.

Border 1

From Fabric 4 cut 4 strips 13¾in x 3¼in (35cm x 8.3cm). Extra fabric is allowed for fussy cutting if desired, to achieve balanced colour shading.
From Fabric 5 cut 4 corner squares 3¼in (8.3cm).

Border 2

From Fabric 7 and Fabric 8, and using Template A, cut 3in (7.6cm) wide strips across the width of the fabric. Each strip will give you 12 triangles per width. Align the template's long side with the long edge of the strip (to avoid a bias edge). From Fabric 7 cut 12 triangles and from Fabric 8 cut 16. Rotate the template 180 degrees alternately for economical cuts.
From Fabric 2 cut 2 squares 7⅞in (20cm). Cut each square in half once diagonally to make 4 of Triangle b.
From Fabric 10 cut 2 squares 7⅞in (20cm). Cut each square in half once diagonally to make 4 of Triangle b.

Border 3

From Fabric 11 cut 4 strips 27in x 4¼in (68.6cm x 10.8cm).
From Fabric 12 cut 4 corner squares 4¼in (10.8cm).

Border 4

For the squares in this border cut 3½in (9cm) wide strips across the width of the fabric. Each strip will give you 11 squares per width. From Fabric 7 cut 7 squares. From Fabric 8 cut 7. From Fabric 13 cut 6. From Fabric 14 cut 6. From Fabric 15 cut 6. Total 32 squares.
From Fabric 9, and using Template B, cut 2¾in (7cm) wide strips across the width of the fabric. Each strip will give you 13 triangles per width. Align the template's long side with the long edge of the strip, rotating the template 180 degrees alternately when you cut.
Total 72 triangles. (Note: The ends of the Border 4 pieced strips are trimmed to fit when the quilt is assembled.)
From Fabric 16 cut 4 corner squares 4¾in (12cm).

Border 5

From Fabric 2 cut 5 strips 4½in (11.4cm) wide across the width of the fabric. Join as necessary and cut 4 strips 43in x 4½in (109.2cm x 11.4cm).

From Fabric 8 cut 4 corner squares 4½in (11.4cm).

Border 6

For the squares in this border cut 3½in (9cm) wide strips across the width of the fabric. Each strip will give you 11 squares per width. From Fabric 8 cut 12 squares. From Fabric 13 cut 12. From Fabric 14 cut 16. From Fabric 3 cut 12. From Fabric 4 cut 12. From Fabric 2 cut 18. From Fabric 5 cut 14. From Fabric 11 cut 16. Total 112 squares.
From Fabric 6, and using Template C, cut 4⅞in (12.4cm) wide strips across the width of the fabric. Each strip will give you 7 triangles per width. Align the template's long side with the long edge of the strip, rotating the template 180 degrees alternately.
Total 40 triangles.
From Fabric 6 cut 16 squares 5⅛in (13cm). Cut each square in half once along the diagonal to make a total of 32 of Triangle c.

Border 7

From Fabric 8 cut 8 strips 3½in (9cm) wide across the width of the fabric. Join as necessary and cut 2 strips 68in x 3½in (172.7cm x 9cm) and 2 strips 74in x 3½in (188cm x 9cm).

Backing

From backing Fabric 17 cut a piece 81in x 81in (206cm x 206cm).

Binding

From Fabric 18 cut 8 strips 2½in (6.4cm) wide across the width of the fabric. Sew together end to end.

MAKING THE QUILT

Use a ¼in (6mm) seam allowance throughout and refer to Diagrams 1 and 2 on page 62 and Diagram 3 on page 63 for fabric placement.

Quilt centre Take the centre square and sew 2 of Triangle a to opposite sides. Add the other 2 Triangle a to the remaining sides.

Border 1 Sew 2 strips to the quilt sides, easing to fit. Sew the corner squares to the ends of the remaining 2 border strips and sew to the quilt, easing to fit.

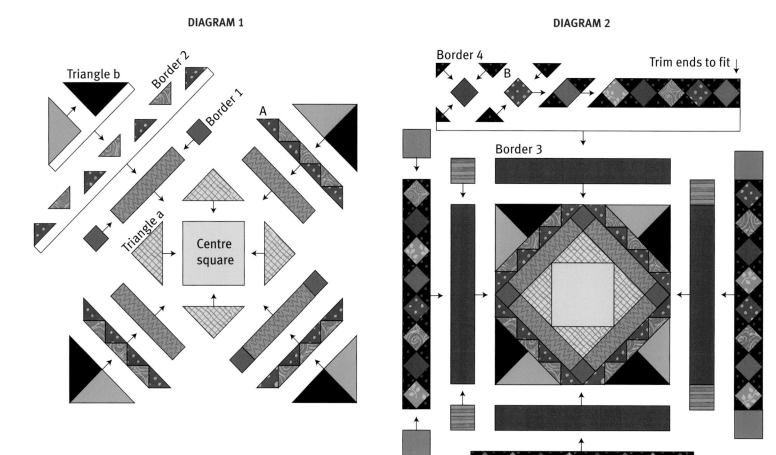

DIAGRAM 1

DIAGRAM 2

Border 2 Using the Template A triangles, piece 4 border strips. Sew them to the quilt sides. Using the Triangle b patches, sew 2 triangles together and sew to a pieced section. Repeat with the other triangles on the remaining sides.

Border 3 Sew 2 strips to the quilt sides. Sew the corner squares to the ends of the remaining 2 border strips and sew to the quilt.

Border 4 Using the 3½in (9cm) squares and the Template B triangles, piece the 4 borders as in Diagram 2. Trim the ends so they fit the quilt. Sew 2 pieced strips to the sides of the quilt. Sew the corner squares to the ends of the remaining 2 pieced strips and sew to the quilt.

Border 5 Sew 2 strips to the quilt sides. Sew the corner squares to the ends of the remaining 2 border strips and sew to the quilt.

Border 6 This border uses 3½in (9cm) squares, Template C triangles and Triangle c patches. Begin by piecing the 4-patch blocks, making a total of 28. Take 6 of the 4-patch blocks and piece them together with the large and small triangles. Follow Diagram 3 or arrange the four-patch blocks randomly. Repeat to make a second pieced unit and then sew these units to the sides of the quilt. Repeat to make another 2 pieced strips, this time with 8 blocks in each. Sew these to the top and bottom of the quilt.

Border 7 Sew the 2 shorter strips to the quilt sides and then the longer strips to the top and bottom.

FINISHING THE QUILT
Press the quilt top.
Layer the quilt top, batting and backing and baste together (see page 148).
Quilt as desired.
Trim the quilt edges and attach the binding (see page 149).

DIAGRAM 3

Border 7

Border 6   C

Triangle c

Triangle c

Border 5

	Fabric 1		Fabric 4		Fabric 7		Fabric 10		Fabric 13		Fabric 16
	Fabric 2		Fabric 5		Fabric 8		Fabric 11		Fabric 14		
	Fabric 3		Fabric 6		Fabric 9		Fabric 12		Fabric 15		

glamping medallion *

Kaffe Fassett

This easy medallion quilt is the perfect opportunity to mix flowery and geometric fabrics to bounce off each other in borders of varying widths, allowing you to practise your border sewing technique at the same time.

SIZE OF FINISHED QUILT
57in x 57in (144.8cm x 144.8cm)

FABRICS
Fabrics calculated at minimum width of 40in (102cm) and are cut across the width, unless otherwise stated. Fabrics have been given a number – see Fabric Swatch Diagram for details.

Patchwork Fabrics

GLAMPING		
Fabric 1	Red	1yd (90cm)
REGIMENTAL STRIPE		
Fabric 2	Red	¼yd (25cm)
Fabric 3	Green	¼yd (25cm)
POMEGRANATE		
Fabric 4	Pink	½yd (45cm)
LOTUS LEAF		
Fabric 5	Citrus	¾yd (70cm)
ROSE CLOUD		
Fabric 6	Aqua	½yd (45cm)
TREFOIL		
Fabric 7	Red	⅞yd (80cm)
JUPITER		
Fabric 8	Red	¼yd (25cm)

Backing and Binding Fabrics

ROSE CLOUD		
Fabric 6	Aqua	3¾yd (3.5m)
JUMBLE		
Fabric 9	Tangerine	½yd (45cm)

Batting
65in x 65in (165cm x 165cm)

CUTTING OUT
Please note that when the border strips are longer than 40in (102cm) – the width of the fabric – you will need to join strips to obtain the required length. Use a ¼in (6mm) seam and press seams open.

Centre Panel
From Fabric 1 cut a square 21½in (54.6cm). Please note that a generous amount of fabric has been allowed in the Fabrics list, so you can centre the fabric design to best effect.

Border 1
From Fabric 3 cut 2 strips 2in x 21½in (5.1cm x 54.6cm) for the top and bottom of the quilt, and 2 strips 2in x 24½in (5.1cm x 62.2cm) for the sides.

Border 2
From Fabric 4 cut 2 strips 3½in x 24½in (9cm x 62.2cm) for the top and bottom of the quilt, and 2 strips 3½in x 30½in (9cm x 77.5cm) for the sides.

Border 3
From Fabric 2 cut 2 strips 2in x 30½in (5cm x 77.5cm) for top and bottom of the quilt and 2 strips 2in x 33½in (5.1cm x 85cm) for the sides.

Border 4
From Fabric 6 cut 2 strips 3½in x 33½in (9cm x 85cm) for the top and bottom of the quilt, and 2 strips 3½in x 39½in (9cm x 100.3cm) for the sides.

Border 5
From Fabric 8 cut 2 strips 2in x 39½in (5.1cm x 100.3cm) for the top and bottom of the quilt, and 2 strips 2in x 42½in (5cm x 108cm) for the sides.

Border 6
From Fabric 5 cut 2 strips 3½in x 42½in (9cm x 108cm) for the top and bottom of the quilt, and 2 strips 3½in x 48½in (9cm x 123.2cm) for the sides.

Border 7
From Fabric 7 cut 2 strips 5in x 48½in (12.7cm x 123.2cm) for the top and bottom of the quilt, and 2 strips 5in x 57½in (12.7cm x 146cm) for the sides.

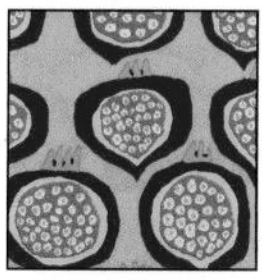

Backing
From backing Fabric 6 cut a piece 40in x 65in (102cm x 165cm) and a piece 26in x 65in (66cm x 165cm).

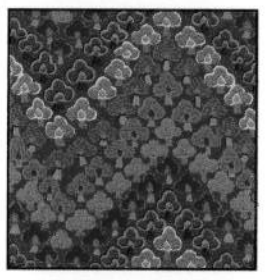

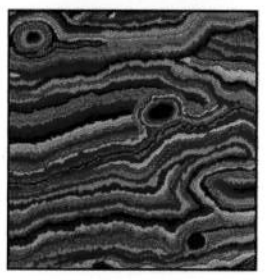

Binding
From Fabric 9 cut 7 strips 2½in (6.4cm) across the width of the fabric. Sew together end to end.

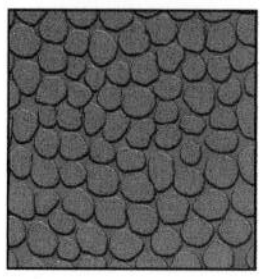

MAKING THE QUILT

Use ¼in (6mm) seams throughout. Refer to Diagram 1 and, starting with Border 1, sew the strips to the centre panel, adding the top and bottom strips first and then the side strips. Press each strip as you add it. Continue in this way, following the piecing order numbers on the diagram, until all 7 borders have been added to the quilt.

FINISHING THE QUILT

Press the quilt top. Sew the backing pieces together using a ¼in (6mm) seam allowance to form a piece approx. 65in (165cm) square.
Layer the quilt top, batting and backing and baste together (see page 148).
Quilt as desired.
Trim the quilt edges and attach the binding (see page 149).

Fabric 1

Fabric 2

Fabric 3

Fabric 4

Fabric 5

Fabric 6

Fabric 7

Fabric 8

DIAGRAM 1

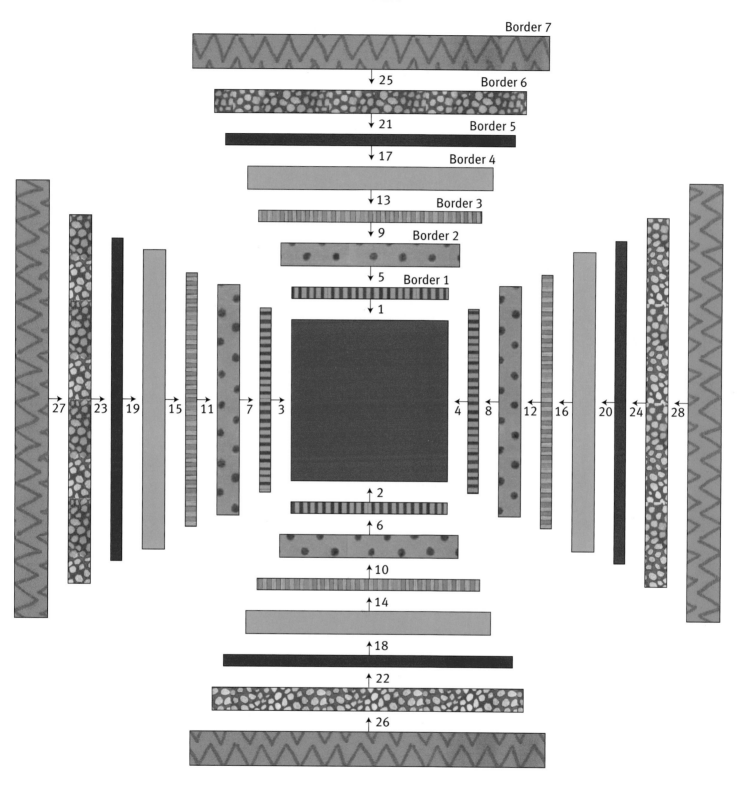

sunny zig zag **

Kaffe Fassett

This is essentially a scrap quilt contrasting yellow fabrics with pink and blue ones. The blocks are made using strip piecing, with varying strip widths used to create a pleasingly random look, arranged in a zig zag pattern. Three different sizes of pieced block borders are alternated with unpieced borders.

FABRIC SWATCH DIAGRAM

Patchwork Fabrics

Fabric 1
END PAPERS
Spring
GP159SP

Fabric 2
JUMBLE
Lemon
BM53LM

Fabric 3
JUMBLE
Pink
BM53PK

Fabric 4
GUINEA FLOWER
Gold
GP59GD

Fabric 5
SPOT
Yellow
GP70YE

Fabric 6
SPOT
Duck Egg
GP70DE

Fabric 7
ABORIGINAL DOT
Purple
GP71PU

Fabric 8
ABORIGINAL DOT
Lime
GP71LM

Fabric 9
ABORIGINAL DOT
Orange
GP71OR

Fabric 10
PAPERWEIGHT
Gold
GP20GD

Fabric 11
ROMAN GLASS
Pink
GP01PK

Fabric 12
ZIG ZAG
Yellow
BM43YE

Fabric 13
ZIG ZAG
Pink
BM43PK

Fabric 14
GOOD VIBRATIONS
Pink
BM65PK

Fabric 15
MOSS
Yellow
BM68YE

Fabric 16
LOTUS LEAF
Jade
GP29JA

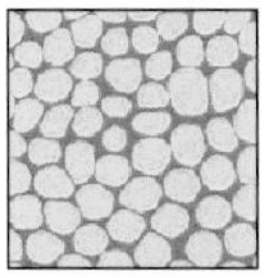

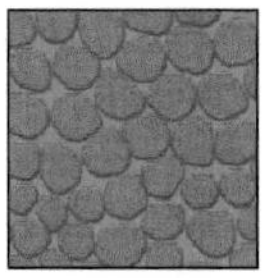

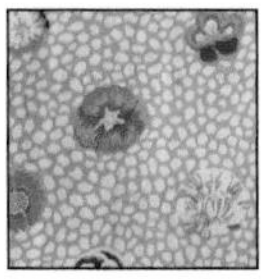

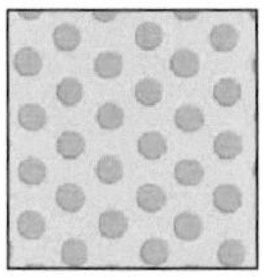

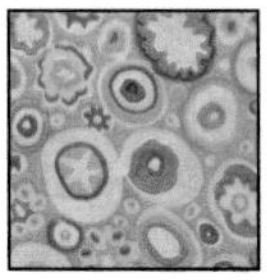

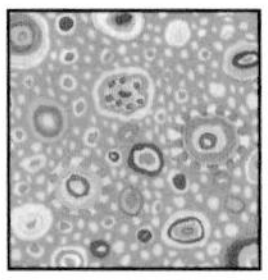

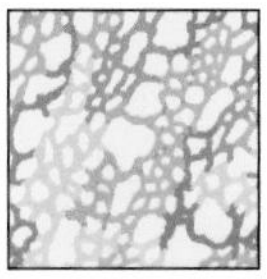

Backing and Binding Fabrics

Fabric 16
LOTUS LEAF
Jade
GP29JA

Fabric 4
GUINEA FLOWER
Gold
GP59GD

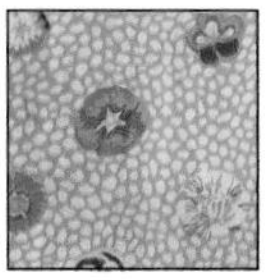

SIZE OF FINISHED QUILT
72in x 72in (183cm x 183cm)

FABRICS
Fabrics calculated at minimum width of 40in (102cm) and are cut across the width, unless otherwise stated. Fabrics have been given a number – see Fabric Swatch Diagram for details.

Patchwork Fabrics
END PAPERS

| Fabric 1 | Spring | ½yd (45cm) |

JUMBLE

| Fabric 2 | Lemon | ¾yd (70cm) |
| Fabric 3 | Pink | ¾yd (70cm) |

GUINEA FLOWER

| Fabric 4 | Gold | ¾yd (70cm) |

SPOT

| Fabric 5 | Yellow | ¾yd (70cm) |
| Fabric 6 | Duck Egg | ¾yd (70cm) |

ABORIGINAL DOT

Fabric 7	Purple	¾yd (70cm)
Fabric 8	Lime	¾yd (70cm)
Fabric 9	Orange	¾yd (70cm)

PAPERWEIGHT

| Fabric 10 | Gold | ¾yd (70cm) |

ROMAN GLASS

| Fabric 11 | Pink | ¾yd (70cm) |

ZIG ZAG

| Fabric 12 | Yellow | ¾yd (70cm) |
| Fabric 13 | Pink | ¾yd (70cm) |

GOOD VIBRATIONS

| Fabric 14 | Pink | ¾yd (70cm) |

Border Fabrics
JUMBLE

| Fabric 2 | Lemon | ¼yd (25cm) |

MOSS

| Fabric 15 | Yellow | ⅜yd (35cm) |

LOTUS LEAF

| Fabric 16 | Jade | ¾yd (70cm) |

Backing and Binding Fabrics
LOTUS LEAF

| Fabric 16 | Jade | 4¾yd (4.4m) |

GUINEA FLOWER

| Fabric 4 | Gold | ⅝yd (60cm) |

Batting
80in x 80in (203cm x 203cm)

Template plastic

CUTTING OUT

Centre block

Make a paper triangle template by cutting a 12¼in (31.1cm) square of paper diagonally into two triangles. From Fabric 1 cut 2 strips, 8¾in (22.2cm) x width of fabric. Place the triangle template with the long edge of the triangle along the long cut edge of the fabric so the pattern on the fabric runs in the same direction on each cut triangle. Cut 4 triangles in total (you will get 2 triangles per strip).

Border 1

From Fabric 2 cut 2 strips 2½in x 16½in (6.4cm x 42cm) and 2 strips 2½in x 20½in (6.4cm x 52cm).

Border 3

From Fabric 15 cut 2 strips 3in x 30½in (7.6cm x 77.5cm) and 2 strips 3in x 35½in (7.6cm x 90.2cm). Reserve leftover fabric for the Strip Set piecing.

Border 5

From Fabric 16 cut 2 strips 4in x 49½in (10.2cm x 125.8cm) and 2 strips 4in x 56½in (10.2cm x 143.5cm), joining strips as necessary.

Strip Sets

The pieced blocks are made by sewing fabric strips into strip-pieced sets, using Fabrics 2 to 14. The fabrics are cut across the full width of the fabric and at varying widths ranging from 1in (2.5cm) up to 2¾in (7cm) in ¼in (6mm) increments.

Backing

From backing Fabric 16 cut 2 pieces 40in x 80in (102cm x 203cm).

Binding

From Fabric 4 cut 8 strips 2½in (6.4cm) across the width of the fabric. Sew together end to end.

MAKING THE PIECED BLOCKS

Use a ¼in (6mm) seam allowance throughout. There are three sizes of pieced square blocks in the quilt – small, medium and large. Use the photograph as a guide to fabric combinations. Here, yellow fabrics are mixed randomly with pink/blue fabrics, alternated where possible, but this quilt is an adventure, so take the idea on your own journey!

Small square block Make a plastic template 5½in (14cm) square. Sew fabric strips together so they make a strip set that is at least 8in (20.3cm) deep (raw edge to raw edge). Press the strip set and cut it into squares by angling the template at 45 degrees, as shown in Diagram 1. Cut a total of 20 small square blocks.

Medium square block Make a plastic template 7½in (19cm) square. Make up strip sets at least 11in (28cm) deep. Using the same technique as for the small square blocks, cut a total of 24 medium square blocks.

Large square block Make a plastic template 8½in (21.5cm) square. Make up strip sets at least 12½in (31.8cm) deep (to the raw edge). Using the same technique as for the small square blocks, cut a total of 32 large square blocks.

MAKING THE CENTRE BLOCK

To make the centre block of the quilt, take the four triangles of Fabric 1 cut earlier and, using ¼in (6mm) seams, sew them together so the fabric's zig zag pattern rotates around the centre, as in Diagram 2. Check that the block is 16½in (42cm) square.

MAKING THE QUILT

Use ¼in (6mm) seams throughout.

Border 1 Add the Border 1 strips to the sides of the quilt first, and then add the top and bottom strips.

Border 2 Make 2 borders of 4 small blocks for the quilt sides, angling the diagonals to form a zig zag as shown in Diagram 2. Sew to the quilt sides. Make 2 borders of 6 small blocks (making a zig zag pattern) and sew to the top and bottom of the quilt.

DIAGRAM 1

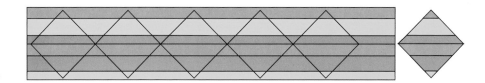

DIAGRAM 2

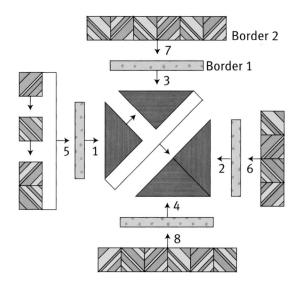

Border 2

7

Border 1

3

5   1

2   6

4

8

DIAGRAM 3

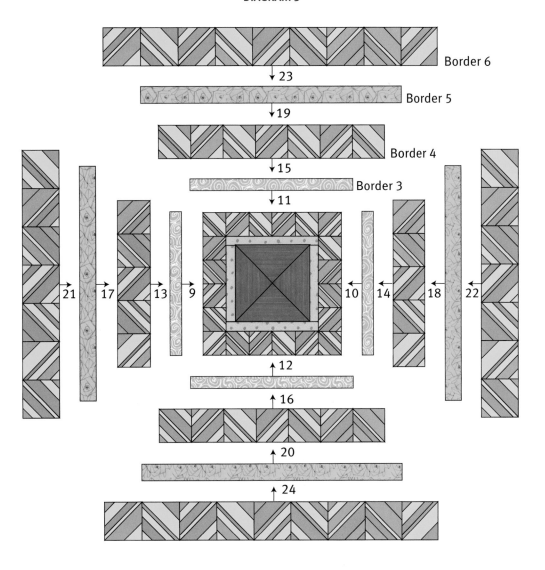

Border 6

↓ 23

Border 5

↓ 19

Border 4

↓ 15

Border 3

↓ 11

21 17 13 9 10 14 18 22

↑ 12

↑ 16

↑ 20

↑ 24

Border 3 Add the Border 3 strips to the sides of the quilt first, and then add the top and bottom strips.

Border 4 Make 2 borders of 5 medium blocks for the quilt sides, angling the diagonals to form a zig zag as before (see Diagram 3). Sew to the quilt sides. Make 2 borders of 7 medium blocks (making a zig zag pattern) and sew to the top and bottom of the quilt.

Border 5 Add the Border 5 strips to the sides of the quilt first, and then add the top and bottom strips.

Border 6 Make 2 borders of 7 large blocks for the quilt sides, angling the diagonals to form a zig zag as before. Sew to the quilt sides. Make 2 borders

of 9 large blocks (making a zig zag pattern) and sew to the top and bottom of the quilt.

FINISHING THE QUILT
Press the quilt top. Sew the backing pieces together using a ¼in (6mm) seam allowance to form a piece approx. 80in (203cm) square.
Layer the quilt top, batting and backing and baste together (see page 148). Quilt as desired.
Trim the quilt edges and attach the binding (see page 149).

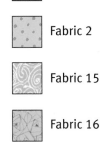

Yellow fabrics 2, 4, 5, 8, 10, 12

Pink fabrics 3, 9, 11, 13, 14

Blue fabrics 6, 7

Fabric 1

Fabric 2

Fabric 15

Fabric 16

71

blue square dance **

Kaffe Fassett

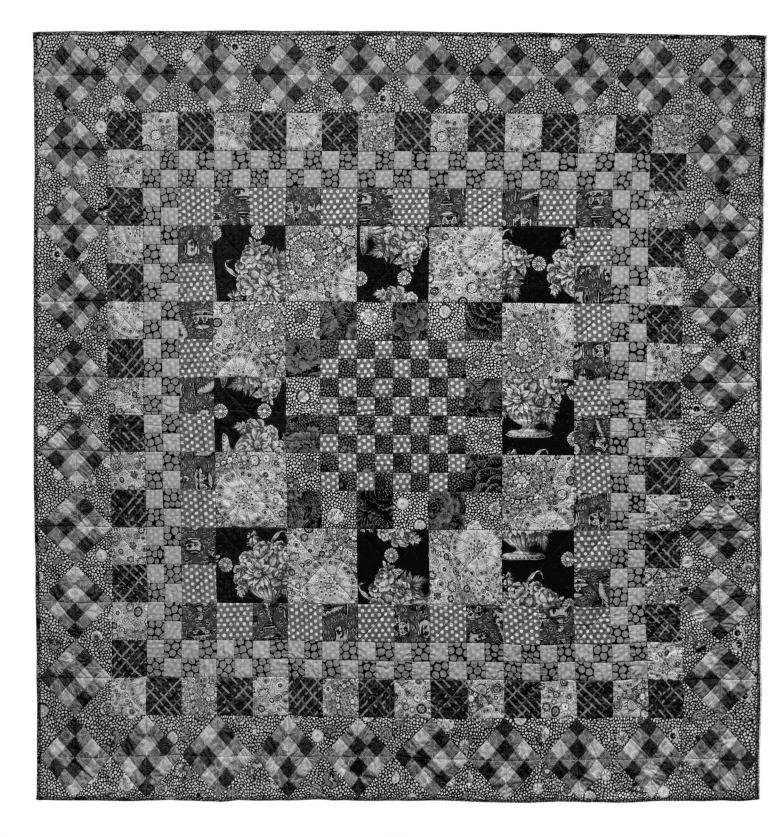

This quilt was inspired by an 18th-century quilt created from blue mattress ticking and red plaids. In this recoloured version, the central checkerboard and five of the six borders are in different shades of blue, with the blue and red combination reserved solely for the outer border.

SIZE OF FINISHED QUILT
80in x 80in (203cm x 203cm)

FABRICS
Fabrics calculated at minimum width of 40in (102cm) and are cut across the width, unless otherwise stated. Fabrics have been given a number – see Fabric Swatch Diagram for details.

Patchwork Fabrics
BRASSICA			
Fabric 1	Blue		³⁄₈yd (40cm)
GUINEA FLOWER			
Fabric 2	Cobalt		¼yd (25cm)
Fabric 3	Blue		1½yd (1.4m)
SPOT			
Fabric 4	China Blue		⅝yd (60cm)
Fabric 5	Duck Egg		⅝yd (60cm)
JUMBLE			
Fabric 6	Duck Egg		⅝yd (60cm)
MILLEFIORE			
Fabric 7	Lilac		1yd (90cm)
ABORIGINAL DOT			
Fabric 8	Lilac		⅞yd (80cm)
Fabric 9	Iris		½yd (45cm)
Fabric 10	Mint		½yd (45cm)
MAD PLAID			
Fabric 11	Cobalt		⅝yd (60cm)
STONE FLOWER			
Fabric 12	Lavender		⅝yd (60cm)
DELFT POTS			
Fabric 13	Blue		½yd (45cm)

Backing and Binding Fabrics
STONE FLOWER			
Fabric 14	Royal		2½yd (2.3m)

of extra-wide fabric (108in/274cm)
GUINEA FLOWER			
Fabric 2	Cobalt		¾yd (70cm)

Batting
88 x 88in (223.5 x 223.5cm)

Patchwork Fabrics

Fabric 1
BRASSICA
Blue
PJ51BL

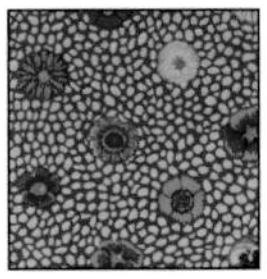

Fabric 2
GUINEA FLOWER
Cobalt
GP59CB

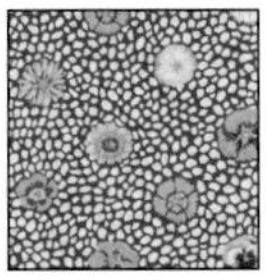

Fabric 3
GUINEA FLOWER
Blue
GP59BL

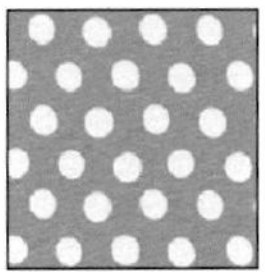

Fabric 4
SPOT
China Blue
GP70CI

Fabric 5
SPOT
Duck Egg
GP70DE

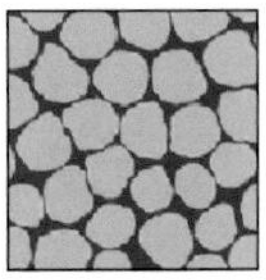

Fabric 6
JUMBLE
Duck Egg
BM53DE

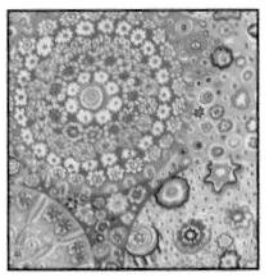

Fabric 7
MILLEFIORE
Lilac
GP92LI

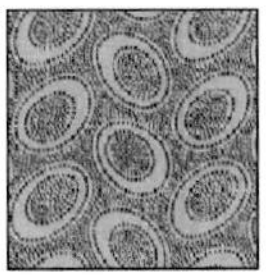

Fabric 8
ABORIGINAL DOT
Lilac
GP71LI

Fabric 9
ABORIGINAL DOT
Iris
GP71IR

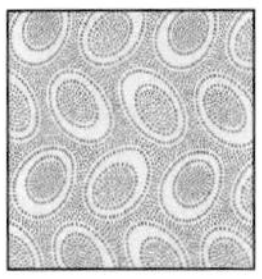

Fabric 10
ABORIGINAL DOT
Mint
GP71MT

Fabric 11
MAD PLAID
Cobalt
BM37CB

Fabric 12
STONE FLOWER
Lavender
GP173LV

Fabric 13
DELFT POTS
Blue
GP165BL

Backing and Binding Fabrics

Fabric 14
STONE FLOWER
Royal
QBGP005RY

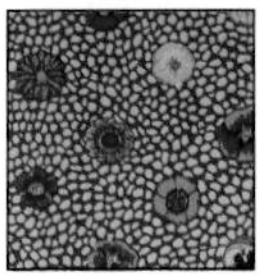

Fabric 2
GUINEA FLOWER
Cobalt
GP59CB

CUTTING OUT
Cut all fabrics from the width of the fabric and then sub-cut as described.

Centre Checkerboard
From Fabric 2 cut two 2½in (6.4cm) wide strips.
From Fabric 4 cut two 2½in (6.4cm) wide strips.
Cut these strips into 2½in (6.4cm) squares, to make 32 squares in each fabric.

Border 1
From Fabric 1 cut 2 strips 4½in (11.4cm) wide.
From Fabric 3 cut 2 strips 4½in (11.4cm) wide.
Cut these strips into 4½in (11.4cm) squares, to make 10 squares in each fabric.

Border 2

From Fabric 12 cut 2 strips 8½in (21.6cm) wide.
From Fabric 7 cut 2 strips 8½in (21.6cm) wide.
Cut these strips into 8½in (21.6cm) squares, to make 8 squares in each fabric.

Border 3

From Fabric 13 cut 3 strips 4½in (11.4cm) wide.
From Fabric 4 cut 3 strips 4½in (11.4cm) wide.
Cut these strips into 4½in (11.4cm) squares, to make 22 squares in each fabric.

Border 4

From Fabric 6 cut 7 strips 2½in (6.4cm) wide.
From Fabric 5 cut 7 strips 2½in (6.4cm) wide.
Cut these strips into 2½in (6.4cm) squares, to make 104 squares in each fabric.

Border 5

From Fabric 11 cut 4 strips 4½in (11.4cm) wide.
From Fabric 7 cut 4 strips 4½in (11.4cm) wide.
Cut these strips into 4½in (11.4cm) squares, to make 30 squares in each fabric.

Border 6

From Fabric 8 cut 15 strips 2in (5.1cm) wide. From these strips, cut 288 squares 2in (5.1cm).
From Fabric 9 cut 8 strips 2in (5.1cm) wide. From these strips, cut 144 squares 2in (5.1cm).
From Fabric 10 cut 8 strips 2in (5.1cm) wide. From these strips, cut 144 squares 2in (5.1cm).
From Fabric 3 cut 10 strips 4⅞in (12.4cm) wide. From these strips cut 72 squares 4⅞in (12.4cm). Cut each square diagonally once to make 2 triangles per square to make 144 triangles.

Backing

From backing Fabric 14, cut a piece 88in x 88in (223.5cm x 223.5cm).

Binding

From binding Fabric 2 cut 10 strips 2½in (6.4cm) wide across the width of the fabric. Sew together end to end.

MAKING THE QUILT

Use a ¼in (6mm) seam allowance throughout. For all borders, sew the side borders in place first and press, and then the top and bottom borders and press. Refer to Diagram 4 (see page 76) for the quilt assembly.

Centre Checkerboard Stitch the 2½in (6.4cm) squares together in 8 alternating rows of 8 squares each (see Diagram 1). Stitch these rows together to form the centre checkerboard. Check the piecing is 16½in (42cm) square.

Border 1 Using the 4½in (11.4cm) squares in an alternating pattern, sew 4 together and sew to the sides of the quilt. Sew 6 together and sew to the top and bottom of the quilt.

Border 2 Using the 8½in (21.6cm) squares in an alternating pattern, sew 3 together and sew to the sides of the quilt. Sew 5 together and sew to the top and bottom of the quilt.

Border 3 Using the 4½in (11.4cm) squares in an alternating pattern, sew 10 together and sew to the sides of the quilt. Sew 12 together and sew to the top and bottom of the quilt.

Border 4 Sew the squares into 52 4-patch blocks, making each block as in Diagram 2. Sew 12 blocks together and sew to the sides of the quilt. Sew 14 blocks together and sew to the top and bottom of the quilt.

Border 5 Using the 4½in (11.4cm) squares, sew 14 squares together and sew to the sides of the quilt. Sew 16 squares together and sew to the top and bottom of the quilt.

Border 6 All of the on-point 16-patch blocks in this border are made in the same way. Lay out sixteen 2in (5.1cm) squares as in Diagram 3 and sew them together in 4 rows each with 4 squares. Now join the rows together. Trim approximately ⅛in (3mm) from each side of the unit so it measures 6⅜in (16.2cm) square. Take 4 of the 4⅞in (12.4cm) triangles and sew 2 to opposite sides of the 16-patch block with right sides together. Press the seams and then sew

DIAGRAM 1

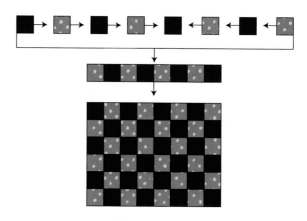

DIAGRAM 2

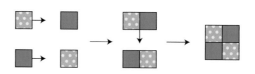

74

DIAGRAM 3

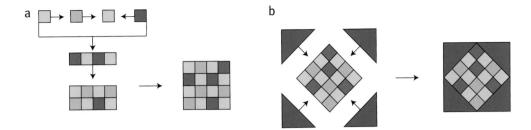

the other 2 triangles on the remaining sides and press. Repeat this to make 36 blocks in total.

Join 8 blocks together for the sides of the quilt and sew in place. Join 10 blocks together for the top and bottom of the quilt and sew in place.

Note: If you rotate the blocks to make each block a different orientation from its neighbour, this will heighten the scrappy effect of the quilt.

FINISHING THE QUILT
Press the quilt top.
Layer the quilt top, batting and backing and baste together (see page 148).
Quilt as desired.
Trim the quilt edges and attach the binding (see page 149).

DIAGRAM 4

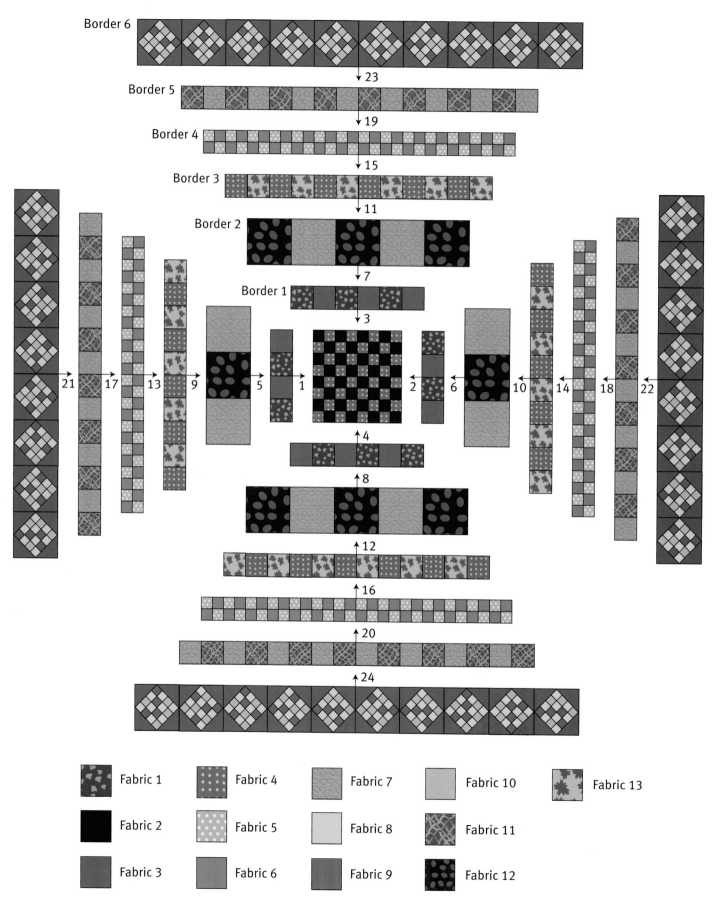

Border 6

Border 5

Border 4

Border 3

Border 2

Border 1

	Fabric 1		Fabric 4		Fabric 7		Fabric 10		Fabric 13
	Fabric 2		Fabric 5		Fabric 8		Fabric 11		
	Fabric 3		Fabric 6		Fabric 9		Fabric 12		

autumn chintz **

Kaffe Fassett

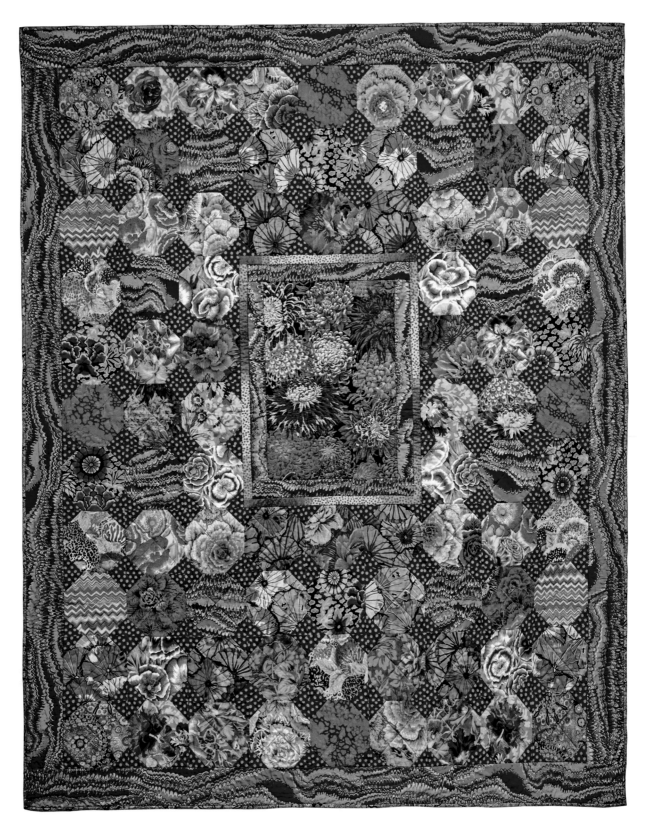

FABRIC SWATCH DIAGRAM

Patchwork Fabrics

Fabric 1
JAPANESE
CHRYSANTHEMUM
Red
PJ41RD

Fabric 2
JAPANESE
CHRYSANTHEMUM
Brown
PJ41BR

Fabric 3
END PAPERS
Purple
GP159PU

Fabric 4
OMBRE
Brown
GP117BR

Fabric 5
BRASSICA
Rust
PJ51RU

Fabric 6
BRASSICA
Brown
PJ51BR

Fabric 7
POPPY GARDEN
ORANGE
PJ95OR

Fabric 8
POPPY GARDEN
Red
PJ95RD

Fabric 9
ORCHID
Brown
PJ92BR

Fabric 10
LADY'S PURSE
Ochre
PJ94OC

Fabric 11
LOTUS LEAF
Umber
GP29UM

Fabric 12
LOTUS LEAF
Mauve
GP29MV

Fabric 13
DREAM
Brown
GP148BR

Fabric 14
ZIG ZAG
Bright
BM43BT

Fabric 15
BAROQUE FLORAL
Brown
PJ90BR

Fabric 16
BAROQUE FLORAL
Blue
PJ90BL

Fabric 17
MOSS
RED
BM68RD

Fabric 18
MILLEFIORE
Brown
GP92BR

Fabric 19
BROCADE PEONY
Autumn
PJ62AU

Fabric 20
SPOT
Royal
GP70RY

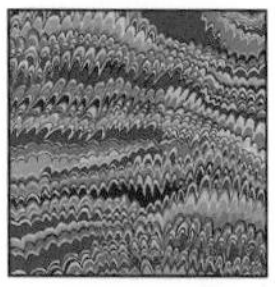

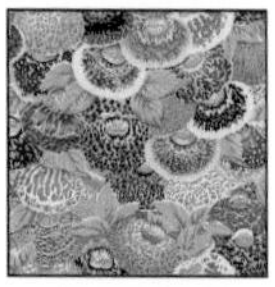

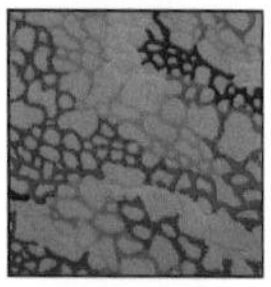

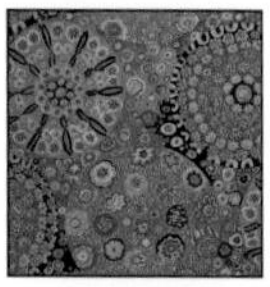

Backing and Binding Fabrics

Fabric 5
BRASSICA
Rust
PJ51RU

Fabric 18
MILLEFIORE
Brown
GP92BR

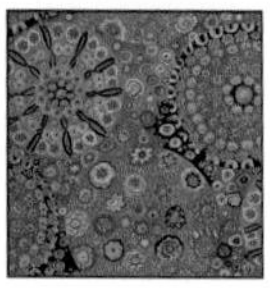

This richly coloured quilt has a Japanese Chrysanthemum centre panel displayed within two borders. The rectangular centre is then surrounded by rows of traditional Snowball blocks. A final border in End Papers, also used for the first border and some of the Snowball blocks, frames the whole design nicely.

SIZE OF FINISHED QUILT
75½in x 90½in (192cm x 230cm)

FABRICS
Fabrics calculated at minimum width of 40in (102cm) and are cut across the width, unless otherwise stated. Fabrics have been given a number – see Fabric Swatch Diagram for details.

Patchwork Fabrics

JAPANESE CHRYSANTHEMUM

Fabric 1	Red	¾yd (70cm)
Fabric 2	Brown	¼yd (25cm)

END PAPERS

Fabric 3	Purple	2yd (1.9m)

OMBRE

Fabric 4	Brown	¼yd (25cm)

BRASSICA

Fabric 5	Rust	¼yd (25cm)
Fabric 6	Brown	½yd (45cm)

POPPY GARDEN

Fabric 7	Orange	½yd (45cm)
Fabric 8	Red	¼yd (25cm)

ORCHID

Fabric 9	Brown	½yd (45cm)

LADY'S PURSE

Fabric 10	Ochre	¼yd (25cm)

LOTUS LEAF

Fabric 11	Umber	½yd (45cm)
Fabric 12	Mauve	½yd (45cm)

DREAM

Fabric 13	Brown	½yd (45cm)

ZIG ZAG

Fabric 14	Bright	¼yd (25cm)

BAROQUE FLORAL

Fabric 15	Brown	½yd (45cm)
Fabric 16	Blue	¼yd (25cm)

MOSS

Fabric 17	Red	¼yd (25cm)

MILLEFIORE

Fabric 18	Brown	¼yd (25cm)

BROCADE PEONY

Fabric 19	Autumn	¼yd (25cm)

SPOT

Fabric 20	Royal	2yd (1.9m)

Backing and Binding Fabrics
BRASSICA
Fabric 5   Rust   6½yd (6m)
MILLEFIORE
Fabric 18   Brown   ¾yd (70cm)

Batting
84in x 99in (213.5cm x 251.5cm)

CUTTING OUT
Centre panel
From Fabric 1 cut a rectangle 17in x 24½in (43.2cm x 62.2cm). Extra fabric has been allowed for fussy cutting if you wish.

Border 1
From Fabric 3 cut 2 strips 24½in x 2½in (62.2cm x 6.4cm) for the sides of the quilt and 2 strips 21in x 2½in (53.3cm x 6.4cm) for the top and bottom.

Border 2
From Fabric 4 cut 2 strips 28½in x 1½in (72.3cm x 3.8cm) for the sides of the quilt and 2 strips 23in x 1½in (58.4cm x 3.8cm) for the top and bottom.

Border 3
From Fabric 3 cut 9 strips 4½in (11.4cm) wide across the width of the fabric. Join as necessary and cut 2 strips 4½in x 83in (11.4cm x 210.8cm) for the sides of the quilt and 2 strips 4½in x 76in (11.4cm x 193cm) for the top and bottom of the quilt.

Block Centres
From Fabric 2, Fabric 3 and Fabrics 5 to 19 (17 fabrics) cut 8in (20.3cm) strips across the width of the fabric. Each strip will give 5 squares per full width. To make the quilt as shown, cut a total of 87 squares, in the following fabrics: Fabric 2 cut 2; Fabric 3 cut 8; Fabric 5 cut 4; Fabric 6 cut 8; Fabric 7 cut 6; Fabric 8 cut 4; Fabric 9 cut 6; Fabric 10 cut 5; Fabric 11 cut 6; Fabric 12 cut 8; Fabric 13 cut 6; Fabric 14 cut 4; Fabric 15 cut 6; Fabric 16 cut 2; Fabric 17 cut 4; Fabric 18 cut 4; Fabric 19 cut 4.

Block Corners
From Fabric 20 cut 25 strips 2¾in (7cm) wide across the width of the fabric. Each strip will give 14 squares per width. Cut a total of 348 squares.

Backing
From backing Fabric 5 cut 2 pieces 40in x 99in (102cm x 251.5cm), 2 pieces 40in x 5in (102cm x 12.7cm) and one piece 20in x 5in (51cm x 12.7cm).

Binding
From binding Fabric 18 cut 9 strips 2½in (6.4cm) wide across the width of the fabric. Sew together end to end.

MAKING THE CENTRE PANEL
Use a ¼in (6mm) seam allowance throughout. Following Diagram 1, take the centre panel and sew a Border 1 side strip to each side. Sew the other Border 1 strips to the top and bottom of the centre panel and press.

Sew the Border 2 border strips in place in the same way.

MAKING THE SNOWBALL BLOCKS
To make the snowball blocks take one large square and 4 small squares. Following the sequence in Diagram 2, place the 4 small squares right sides together onto each corner of the large square, matching the edges carefully (a). Stitch diagonally across the small squares as shown and trim the corners to a ¼in (6mm) seam allowance (b). Press the corners outwards (c).
Make 87 blocks in total.

DIAGRAM 1

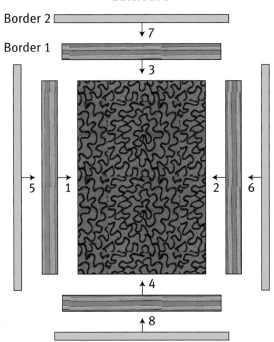

DIAGRAM 2

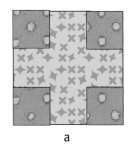 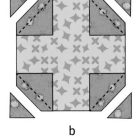 

a   b   c

MAKING THE QUILT

Use a ¼in (6mm) seam allowance throughout. Lay out all the blocks as shown in Diagram 3. Piece the snowball blocks into sections as shown. Join these sections to the centre panel. Finally, add Border 3, adding the side strips first and then the top and bottom strips.

FINISHING THE QUILT

Press the quilt top. Sew the backing pieces together using a ¼in (6mm) seam allowance. Sew the 40in x 5in (102cm x 12.7cm) pieces and the 20in x 5in (51cm x 12.7cm) piece together into a long narrow strip. Sew this between the two larger pieces to form a backing approx. 84in x 99in (213.5cm x 251.5cm).
Layer the quilt top, batting and backing and baste together (see page 148).
Quilt as desired.
Trim the quilt edges and attach the binding (see page 149).

	Fabric 1		Fabric 11
	Fabric 2		Fabric 12
	Fabric 3		Fabric 13
	Fabric 4		Fabric 14
	Fabric 5		Fabric 15
	Fabric 6		Fabric 16
	Fabric 7		Fabric 17
	Fabric 8		Fabric 18
	Fabric 9		Fabric 19
	Fabric 10		Fabric 20

DIAGRAM 3

Border 3

sunny beyond the border *

Brandon Mably

This easy quilt is the perfect way to showcase some gorgeous fabrics. The quilt is assembled from the centre outwards, using a selection of strips cut to size. Fabric amounts given are generous to allow for pattern matching.

SIZE OF FINISHED QUILT
76in x 84in (193cm x 213.5cm)

FABRICS
Fabrics calculated at minimum width of 40in (102cm) and are cut across the width, unless otherwise stated. Fabrics have been given a number – see Fabric Swatch Diagram for details.

Patchwork Fabrics

DELFT POTS			
Fabric 1	Yellow	1yd (90cm)	
STONE FLOWER			
Fabric 2	Orange	½yd (45cm)	
JUMBLE			
Fabric 3	Gold	1yd (90cm)	
ZIG ZAG			
Fabric 4	Multi	¼yd (25cm)	
POMEGRANATE			
Fabric 5	Pink	¼yd (25cm)	
Fabric 6	Yellow	2¼yd (2m)	
ENCHANTED			
Fabric 7	Yellow	⅝yd (60cm)	
SCUBA			
Fabric 8	Yellow	1¼yd (1.2m)	
GLAMPING			
Fabric 9	Yellow	2¼yd (2m)	
MOSS			
Fabric 10	Yellow	¼yd (25cm)	

Backing and Binding Fabrics

SUNBURST			
Fabric 11	Yellow	5¼yd (4.8m)	
JUMBLE			
Fabric 3	Gold	¾yd (70cm)	

Batting
84in x 92in (213.5cm x 233.5cm)

CUTTING OUT

This quilt is assembled from the centre out using a selection of strips (cut to size). To get the look of Brandon's quilt some of the fabrics are cut down the length of the fabric and others across the width, with a bit of pattern matching and joining, so please read the cutting instructions carefully before you start.

Piece A From Fabric 1 and cutting from the length of the fabric, fussy cut a strip 8½in x 32½in (21.6cm x 82.5cm).
Piece B From Fabric 2 cut 2 strips 6½in x 32½in (16.5cm x 82.5cm).
Piece C From Fabric 3 cut 2 strips 6½in x 20½in (16.5cm x 52cm).
Piece D From Fabric 3 cut a strip 6½in x 26½in (16.5 cm x 67.3cm).
Piece E From Fabric 5 cut a strip 6½in x 8½in (16.5cm x 21.6cm).
Piece F From Fabric 4 cut a strip 6½in x 10½in (16.5cm x 26.7cm).
Piece G From Fabric 3 cut a strip 6½in x 32½in (16.5cm x 82.5cm).
Piece H From Fabric 4 cut a square 6½in (16.5cm).
Piece I From Fabric 5 cut a square 6½in (16.5cm).
Piece J From Fabric 8 cut a strip 6½in x 32½in (16.5cm x 82.5cm).
Piece K From Fabric 8 cut a strip 8½in x 50½in (21.6cm x 128.3cm). To obtain the length required, join 2 strips, pattern matching when you join them.
Piece L From Fabric 8 cut a strip 6½in x 40½in (16.5cm x 103cm).
Piece M From Fabric 7 cut a strip 8½in x 56½in (21.6cm x 143.5cm). To obtain the length required, join 2 strips, pattern matching when you join them.
Piece N From Fabric 9 cut a strip 6½in x 40½in (16.5cm x 103cm).
Piece O From Fabric 3 cut a strip 6½in x 8½in (16.5cm x 21.6cm).
Piece P From Fabric 9 cut a strip 6½in x 48½in (16.5cm x 123.2cm). To obtain the length required, join 2 strips, pattern matching when you join them.
Piece Q From Fabric 9 and cutting down the length of the fabric, cut 2 strips 6½in x 68½in (16.5cm x 174cm).
Piece R From Fabric 6 and cutting down the length of the fabric, cut 2 strips 8½in x 68½in (21.6cm x 174cm).
Piece S From Fabric 6 cut 2 strips 8½in x 60½in (21.6cm x 153.7cm). To

obtain the length required, join 2 strips for each Piece S, pattern matching when you join them.
Piece T From Fabric 10 cut 4 squares 8½in (21.6cm).
Backing From Fabric 11 cut 2 pieces 40in x 92in (102cm x 233.7cm).
Binding From binding Fabric 3 cut 9 strips 2½in (6.4cm) wide across the width of the fabric. Sew together end to end.

MAKING THE QUILT

Use a ¼in (6mm) seam allowance throughout. Assemble the quilt in the order indicated in Diagram 1. Follow the

piecing order numbers on the diagram carefully as the piecing order varies.

FINISHING THE QUILT

Press the quilt top. Sew the backing pieces together using a ¼in (6mm) seam allowance and trim to make a piece approx. 84in x 92in (213.5cm x 233.7cm).
Layer the quilt top, batting and backing and baste together (see page 148).
Quilt as desired.
Trim the quilt edges and attach the binding (see page 149).

Patchwork Fabrics

FABRIC SWATCH DIAGRAM

Fabric 1
DELFT POTS
Yellow
GP165YE

Fabric 2
STONE FLOWER
Orange
GP173OR

Fabric 3
JUMBLE
Gold
BM53GD

Fabric 4
ZIG ZAG
Multi
BM43MU

Fabric 5
POMEGRANATE
Pink
BM67PK

Fabric 6
POMEGRANATE
Yellow
BM67YE

Fabric 7
ENCHANTED
Yellow
GP172YE

Fabric 8
SCUBA
Yellow
BM64YE

Fabric 9
GLAMPING
Yellow
BM66YE

Fabric 10
MOSS
Yellow
BM68YE

Backing and Binding Fabrics

Fabric 11
SUNBURST
Yellow
GP162YE

Fabric 3
JUMBLE
Gold
BM53GD

DIAGRAM 1

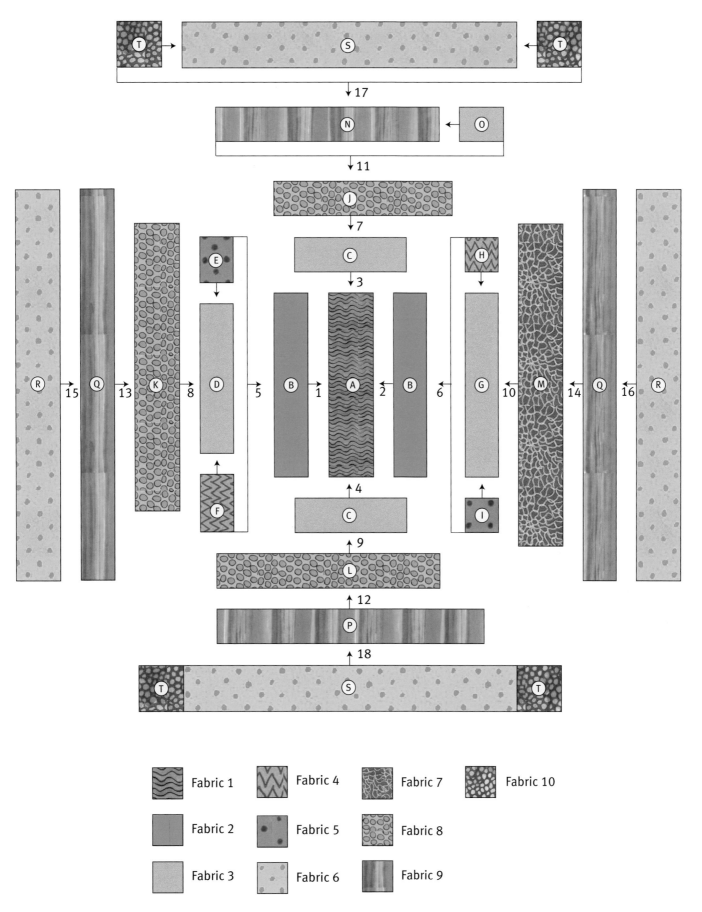

Fabric 1

Fabric 2

Fabric 3

Fabric 4

Fabric 5

Fabric 6

Fabric 7

Fabric 8

Fabric 9

Fabric 10

flowery jar ***

Kaffe Fassett

This bright medallion quilt has six borders surrounding a central panel that features a hand-appliquéd ginger jar. Three of the borders are unpieced and three are pieced, and all of the borders have fussy-cut corner squares.

SIZE OF FINISHED QUILT
80in x 80in (203cm x 203cm)

FABRICS
Fabrics calculated at minimum width of 40in (102cm) and are cut across the width, unless otherwise stated. Fabrics have been given a number – see Fabric Swatch Diagram on page 88 for details.

Patchwork Fabrics

POPPY GARDEN		
Fabric 1	Pink	¾yd (70cm)
ABORIGINAL DOT		
Fabric 2	Lilac	⅝yd (60cm)
LADY'S PURSE		
Fabric 3	Antique	1¼yd (1.2m)
Fabric 4	Red	¼yd (25cm)
BIG BLOOMS		
Fabric 5	Green	¾yd (70cm)
SPOT		
Fabric 6	Duck Egg	¼yd (25cm)
GOOD VIBRATIONS		
Fabric 7	Pink	1½yd (1.4m)
BAROQUE FLORAL		
Fabric 8	Lavender	¾yd (70cm)
ORCHID		
Fabric 9	Blue	¾yd (70cm)
BRASSICA		
Fabric 10	Red	½yd (45cm)
SUCCULENT		
Fabric 11	Pink	¼yd (25cm)
DREAM		
Fabric 12	Aqua	¾yd (70cm)

Backing and Binding Fabrics

LADY'S PURSE		
Fabric 4	Red	5yd (4.6m)
SPOT		
Fabric 13	Grape	⅝yd (60cm)

Batting
88in x 88in (223.5cm x 223.5cm)

Freezer paper
20in x 20in (51cm x 51cm)

TEMPLATES

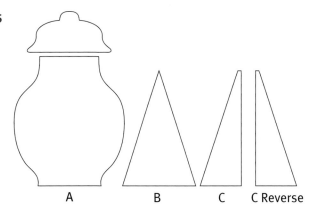

A   B   C   C Reverse

PATCH SHAPES
The quilt is formed around a central panel surrounded by 6 borders. The central panel is square with a hand-appliquéd jar. Note that the appliqué jar and lid templates (A) are printed at 50% of actual size on page 138, so need to be enlarged by 200% on a photocopier. These shapes do not include a seam allowance as they are sewn using a freezer paper method. Borders 1, 3 and 5 are unpieced borders with added corner squares. Borders 2, 4 and 6 are pieced, with added corner squares. Border 6 uses templates B, C and C Reverse, which are given at full size and include seam allowances.

CUTTING OUT
Please note that when the unpieced border strips are longer than 40in (102cm) (width of the fabric), you will need to join strips to obtain the required length. Use a ¼in (6mm) seam and press seams open. On this quilt all corner squares were fussy cut to centre a flower motif within the square where possible.

Centre Panel
From Fabric 2 cut a square 18½in (47cm).

Appliqué Shapes
Cut each template (a jar and a lid) in freezer paper. Press the shiny side of the paper shapes onto the reverse of Fabric 1 and cut out ¼in (6mm) outside of the freezer paper shape.

Border 1
From Fabric 3 cut 4 strips 4in x 18½in (10.2cm x 47cm).
From Fabric 5 fussy cut 4 squares 4in (10.2cm) for corner squares.

Border 2
From Fabric 4, Fabric 6, Fabric 7 and Fabric 8 cut 5 squares 5⅞in (15cm) from each fabric. Cut each square in half along the diagonal once, to make a total of 40 triangles.
From Fabric 1 fussy cut 4 squares 5½in (14cm) for corner squares.

Border 3
From Fabric 12 cut 4 strips 5½in x 35½in (14cm x 90.2cm). From Fabric 1 fussy cut 4 squares 5½in (14cm) for corner squares.

Border 4
From Fabric 5, Fabric 7, Fabric 8 and Fabric 10 cut 6 squares 8⅜in (21.3cm) from each fabric. Cut each square in half along the diagonal once, to make a total of 48 triangles.
From Fabric 11 fussy cut 4 squares 8in (20.3cm) for corner squares.

Border 5
From Fabric 9 cut 4 strips 4½in x 60½in (11.4cm x 153.7cm).
From Fabric 5 fussy cut 4 squares 4½in (11.4cm) for corner squares.

Border 6
From Fabric 3 cut 68 triangles and from Fabric 7 cut 64 triangles using Template B. For the most economical use of the fabric, rotate the template 180 degrees alternately along a fabric strip.
From Fabric 7 cut 4 triangles using Template C and 4 triangles using Template C Reverse.
From Fabric 1 fussy cut 4 squares 6½in (16.5cm) for corner squares.

FABRIC SWATCH DIAGRAM

Patchwork Fabrics

Fabric 1
POPPY GARDEN
Pink
PJ95PK

Fabric 6
SPOT
Duck Egg
GP70DE

Fabric 11
SUCCULENT
Pink
PJ91PK

Fabric 2
ABORIGINAL DOT
Lilac
GP71LI

Fabric 7
GOOD VIBRATIONS
Pink
BM65PK

Fabric 12
DREAM
Aqua
GP148AQ

Fabric 3
LADY'S PURSE
Antique
PJ94AN

Fabric 8
BAROQUE FLORAL
Lavender
PJ90LV

Fabric 4
LADY'S PURSE
Red
PJ94RD

Fabric 9
ORCHID
Blue
PJ92BL

Backing and Binding Fabrics

Fabric 4
LADY'S PURSE
Red
PJ94RD

Fabric 5
BIG BLOOMS
Green
GP91GN

Fabric 10
BRASSICA
Red
PJ51RD

Fabric 13
SPOT
Grape
GP70GP

Backing

From backing Fabric 4 cut 2 pieces 40in x 88in (102cm x 223.5cm) and 1 piece 8in x 88in (20.3cm x 223.5cm).

Binding

From Fabric 13 cut 8 strips 2½in (6.4cm) across the width of the fabric. Sew together end to end.

MAKING THE QUILT

Use a ¼in (6mm) seam allowance throughout and refer to Diagram 1 and Diagram 2 (see page 90) for assembly and fabric placement.

Making the Centre Panel Working first on the fabric pieces for the appliqué jar, press the seam allowance to the reverse of the fabric and baste all around (except the top edge as this will be covered by the lid). Snip the seam allowance at curves and points to help it lie flat. Carefully position the jar on the background (leaving room for the lid) and appliqué the jar into place with invisible stitches. Appliqué the lid in the same way, slightly overlapping the jar. Turn the panel to the reverse and carefully cut away the backing behind the appliqué to within ¼in (6mm) of the stitching line. Carefully remove the basting threads and peel off the freezer paper.

Adding Border 1 Refer to Diagram 1 for fabric placement. Add Border 1 as shown in the diagram, adding the side strips first. For the top and bottom strips, add a corner square to each end first, and then sew the pieced strips into place.

Adding Border 2 For Border 2 take the 5⅞in (15cm) triangles cut earlier and pair them up so the Fabric 4 and Fabric 6 triangles are together and the Fabric 7 and Fabric 8 triangles are together. Sew the triangles together along the diagonal edge to make a total of 20 half-square triangle blocks.
Arrange the blocks as shown in Diagram 1, sewing 4 rows, each with 5 blocks. Add 2 borders to the sides of the quilt. For the top and bottom borders, add a corner square to each end first, and then sew the pieced strips into place.

Adding Border 3 Add Border 3 as shown in Diagram 1, adding the side strips first.

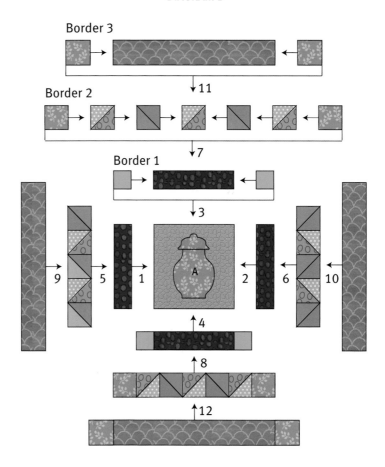

DIAGRAM 1

For the top and bottom strips, add a corner square to each end first, and then sew the pieced strips into place.

Adding Border 4 For Border 4 take the 8⅜in (21.3cm) triangles cut earlier and pair them up so the Fabric 5 and Fabric 10 triangles are together and the Fabric 7 and Fabric 8 triangles are together. Sew the triangles together along the diagonal edge to make a total of 24 half-square triangle blocks.
Arrange the blocks as shown in Diagram 2, sewing 4 rows, each with 6 blocks. Add 2 borders to the sides of the quilt. For the top and bottom borders, add a corner square to each end first, and then sew the pieced strips into place.

Adding Border 5 Add Border 5 as shown in Diagram 2, adding the side strips first. For the top and bottom strips, add a corner square to each end first, and then sew the pieced strips into place.

Adding Border 6 Take 17 of the Fabric 3 (B) triangles and 16 of the Fabric 7 (B) triangles and arrange them alternately in a row as in Diagram 2. Sew the triangles together, offsetting the seams by ¼in (6mm) at each end (see Diagram 3 on page 90). Add a narrow Fabric 7 triangle (C) to one end and a shape C Reverse to the other end. Repeat this pieced strip 4 times in total.
Add 2 of these borders to the sides of the quilt. For the top and bottom borders, add a corner square to each end first, and then sew the pieced strips into place.

FINISHING THE QUILT

Press the quilt top. Sew the backing pieces together using a ¼in (6mm) seam allowance to form a piece approx. 88in (223.5cm) square.
Layer the quilt top, batting and backing and baste together (see page 148).
Quilt as desired.
Trim the quilt edges and attach the binding (see page 149).

DIAGRAM 2

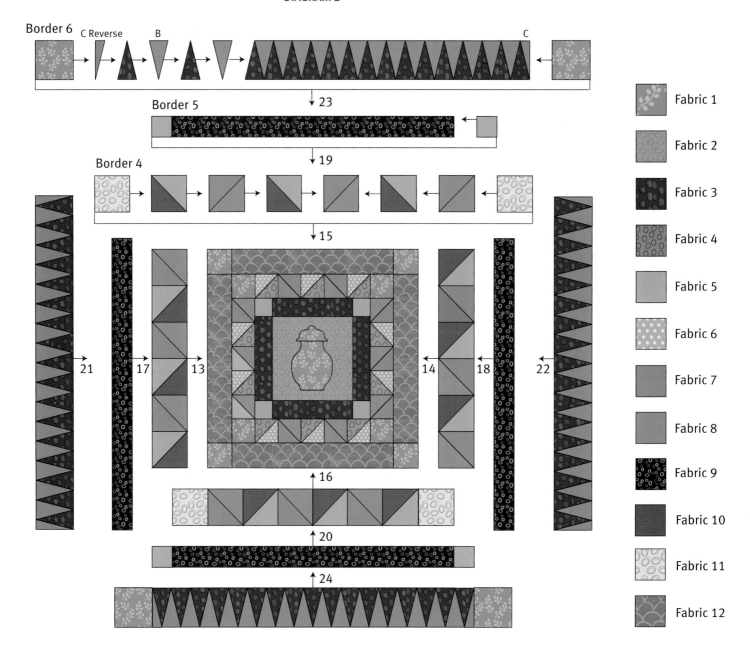

Border 6

C Reverse   B   C

Border 5

Border 4

Fabric 1
Fabric 2
Fabric 3
Fabric 4
Fabric 5
Fabric 6
Fabric 7
Fabric 8
Fabric 9
Fabric 10
Fabric 11
Fabric 12

DIAGRAM 3

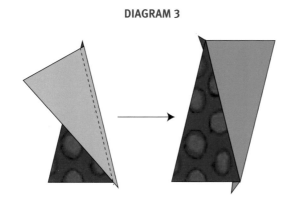

90

autumn checkerboard ***

Liza Prior Lucy

This medallion quilt has been made in two different colourways (see Graphite Medallion on page 96). This version, in warm autumn colours, has eight borders around a centre Snowball block. An interesting variety of other blocks are used to create the pieced borders.

SIZE OF FINISHED QUILT
78in x 78in (198cm x 198cm)

FABRICS
Fabrics calculated at minimum width of 40in (102cm) and are cut across the width, unless otherwise stated. Fabrics have been given a number – see Fabric Swatch Diagram for details.

Patchwork Fabrics
ENCHANTED
Fabric 1   Dark   1¾yd (1.6m)
SPOT
Fabric 2   Bottle   1½yd (1.4m)
Fabric 3   Plum   1yd (90cm)
MILLEFIORE
Fabric 4   Antique   ⅜yd (40cm)
ABORIGINAL DOT
Fabric 5   Periwinkle ½yd (45cm)
Fabric 6   Plum   ¼yd (25cm)
Fabric 7   Charcoal   ⅜yd (40cm)
Fabric 8   Orchid   ½yd (45cm)
TIDDLYWINKS
Fabric 9   Blue   ½yd (45cm)
PAPERWEIGHT
Fabric 10   Purple   ⅜yd (40cm)
Fabric 11   Jewel   ⅜yd (40cm)
JAPANESE CHRYSANTHEMUM
Fabric 12   Autumn   ¾yd (70cm)

Backing and Binding Fabrics
FULL BLOWN
Fabric 13   Red   2½yd (2.25m)
of extra-wide fabric (108in/274cm)
ABORIGINAL DOT
Fabric 6   Plum   ¾yd (70cm)

Batting
86in x 86in (218.5cm x 218.5cm)

FABRIC SWATCH DIAGRAM

Patchwork Fabrics

Fabric 1
ENCHANTED
Dark
GP172DK

Fabric 2
SPOT
Bottle
GP70BT

Fabric 3
SPOT
Plum
GP70PL

Fabric 4
MILLEFIORE
Antique
GP92AN

Fabric 5
ABORIGINAL DOT
Periwinkle
GP71PE

Fabric 6
ABORIGINAL DOT
Plum
GP71PL

Fabric 7
ABORIGINAL DOT
Charcoal
GP71CC

Fabric 8
ABORIGINAL DOT
Orchid
GP71OD

Fabric 9
TIDDLYWINKS
Blue
GP171BL

Fabric 10
PAPERWEIGHT
Purple
GP20PU

Fabric 11
PAPERWEIGHT
Jewel
GP20JE

Fabric 12
JAPANESE CHRYSANTHEMUM
Autumn
PJ41AU

Backing and Binding Fabrics

Fabric 13
FULL BLOWN
Red
QBGP004RD

Fabric 6
ABORIGINAL DOT
Plum
GP71PL

CUTTING OUT
Cut fabrics from the width of the fabric and then sub-cut as described. Some of the fabrics are fussy cut.

Centre Panel
From Fabric 1 fussy cut a 12½in (31.8cm) square, centring on a large bloom of your choice.
From Fabric 2 cut 4 squares 3½in (9cm) for corner triangles.

Border 1
From Fabric 2 cut 2 strips 2in (5.1cm) wide across the width of the fabric. Sub-cut 2 strips 2in x 12½in (5.1cm x 31.8cm) and 2 strips 2in x 15½in (5.1cm x 39.4cm).

Border 2
From Fabric 2 cut 4 squares 3½in (9cm) for corner squares.
From Fabric 4 cut 28 squares 3½in (9cm).
From Fabric 5 cut 8 squares 3½in (9cm).
From Fabric 6 cut 16 squares 3½in (9cm).

Border 3

From Fabric 9 cut 4 strips 3½in x 27½in (9cm x 70cm). Fussy cut these strips to ensure the circles are straight.
From Fabric 2 cut 4 squares 3½in (9cm) for corner squares.

Border 4

From Fabric 7 cut 24 squares 3½in (9cm).
From Fabric 10 cut 24 squares 3½in (9cm).

Border 5

From Fabric 8 cut 112 squares 2⅜in (6cm). Cut each square diagonally once to make 2 triangles per square.
Total 224 triangles.
From Fabric 11 cut 56 squares 2⅝in (6.7cm).

Border 6

From Fabric 5 cut 5 strips 2in (5.1cm) wide across the width of the fabric. Join as necessary and then cut 2 strips 2in x 45½in (5.1cm x 115.6cm) and 2 strips 2in x 48½in (5.1cm x 123.2cm).

Border 7

From Fabric 12 cut 36 squares 4¾in (12cm).
From Fabric 3 cut 14 squares 7⅛in (18cm). Cut each square diagonally both ways to make 4 triangles per square.
Total 56 triangles.
From Fabric 3 cut 16 squares 3⅞in (9.8cm). Cut each square diagonally once to make 2 triangles per square.
Total 32 triangles.

Border 8

From Fabric 1 cut 3½in (9cm) strips across the width of the fabric. Each strip will give you 11 squares. Cut 138 squares.
From Fabric 2 cut 3½in (9cm) strips across the width of the fabric.
Cut 138 squares.

Backing

From Fabric 13 cut a piece 86in x 86in (218.5cm x 218.5cm).

Binding

From binding Fabric 6 cut 9 strips 2½in (6.4cm) wide across the width of the fabric. Sew together end to end.

MAKING THE QUILT

Use a ¼in (6mm) seam allowance throughout. Follow Diagrams 1 to 6 for the piecing, colour placement and quilt layout.

Centre Panel Place the four 3½in (9cm) squares right side down on the large square. Sew across the diagonals of the small squares, trim excess fabric and press the triangles outwards (Diagram 1).

Border 1 Sew the short border strips to the sides of the quilt and the longer strips to the top and bottom.

Border 2 Sew the 3½in (9cm) squares together in pairs in the pattern shown in Diagram 2. Make 2 sections of 2 x 5 squares and sew to the sides of the quilt. Make 2 sections of 2 x 9 squares and sew to the top and bottom.

Border 3 Sew 2 border strips to the sides of the quilt. For the top and bottom strips, add a corner square to each end first, and then sew in place.

Border 4 Sew the 3½in (9cm) squares together in the alternating pattern shown in Diagram 6. Make 2 sections of 11 squares and sew to the sides of the quilt. Make 2 sections of 13 squares and sew to the top and bottom.

Border 5 Follow Diagram 3 to piece this border. Take a 2⅝in (6.7cm) square and 4 triangles 2⅜in (6cm). Sew 2 triangles to the sides of the square and then add the other two triangles. Repeat to make 56 blocks. Sew 13 blocks together for the sides of the quilt. Sew 15 blocks together for the top and bottom of the quilt.

Border 6 Sew the shorter border strips to the sides of the quilt. Sew the longer strips to the top and bottom.

Border 7 Follow Diagram 4 to piece this border. Sew 2 of the larger triangles to the sides of a square. Repeat as shown in the diagram. Sew the segments together into rows. Add the smaller triangles to the end of the rows, as shown. Sew the 4 corner blocks together in the same way as the blocks in Border 5.

DIAGRAM 1

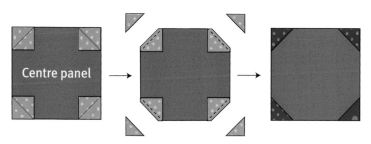

DIAGRAM 2

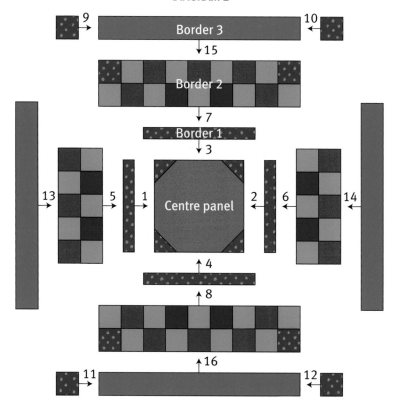

DIAGRAM 3

DIAGRAM 4

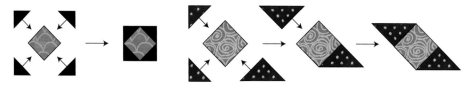

DIAGRAM 5

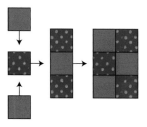

DIAGRAM 6

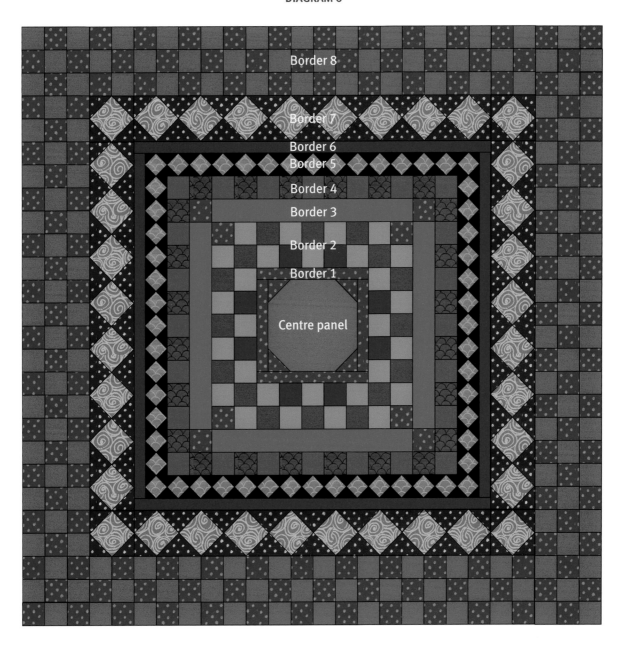

Border 8 Sew the 3½in (9cm) squares together in the alternating pattern shown in Diagram 5. Make 2 sections of 3 x 20 squares and sew to the sides of the quilt. Make 2 sections of 3 x 26 squares and sew to the top and bottom.

FINISHING THE QUILT
Press the quilt top. Layer the quilt top, batting and backing and baste together (see page 148).
Quilt as desired.
Trim the quilt edges and attach the binding (see page 149).

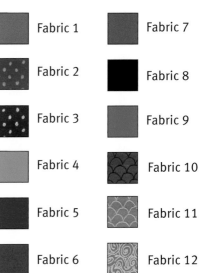

Fabric 1

Fabric 2

Fabric 3

Fabric 4

Fabric 5

Fabric 6

Fabric 7

Fabric 8

Fabric 9

Fabric 10

Fabric 11

Fabric 12

graphite medallion ***

Kaffe Fassett

This quilt uses mostly cool shades and is almost identical to Autumn Checkerboard (see page 91) except this version has an extra fabric added. The layout is the same, apart from a slightly different arrangement of the squares in Border 2.

SIZE OF FINISHED QUILT
78in x 78in (198cm x 198cm)

FABRICS
Fabrics calculated at minimum width of 40in (102cm) and are cut across the width, unless otherwise stated. Fabrics have been given a number – see Fabric Swatch Diagram for details.

Patchwork Fabrics
JAPANESE CHRYSANTHEMUM
Fabric 1	Contrast	1¾yd (1.6m)

SPOT
Fabric 2	Charcoal	1½yd (1.4m)

JUMBLE
Fabric 3	Turquoise	1yd (90cm)

CREASED
Fabric 4	Turquoise	⅜yd (40cm)

MAD PLAID
Fabric 5	Contrast	¼yd (25cm)

ZIG ZAG
Fabric 6	Contrast	¼yd (25cm)

ABORIGINAL DOT
Fabric 7	Purple	⅜yd (40cm)

DIAMOND STRIPE
Fabric 8	Dark	½yd (45cm)

STONE FLOWER
Fabric 9	Turquoise	½yd (45cm)

ROW FLOWERS
Fabric 10	Contrast	⅜yd (40cm)

SPOT
Fabric 11	Silver	⅜yd (40cm)

ENCHANTED
Fabric 12	Grey	¾yd (70cm)

TIDDLYWINKS
Fabric 13	Contrast	⅜yd (40cm)

Backing and Binding Fabrics
STONE FLOWER
Fabric 14	Grey	2½yd (2.25m)

of extra-wide fabric (108in/274cm)
CREASED
Fabric 4	Turquoise	¾yd (70cm)

Batting
86in x 86in (218.5cm x 218.5cm)

FABRIC SWATCH DIAGRAM

Patchwork Fabrics

Fabric 1
JAPANESE
CHRYSANTHEMUM
Contrast
PJ41CT

Fabric 2
SPOT
Charcoal
GP70CC

Fabric 3
JUMBLE
Turquoise
BM53TQ

Fabric 4
CREASED
Turquoise
BM50TQ

Fabric 5
MAD PLAID
Contrast
BM37CT

Fabric 6
ZIG ZAG
Contrast
BM43CT

Fabric 7
ABORIGINAL DOT
Purple
GP71PU

Fabric 8
DIAMOND STRIPE
Dark
GP170DK

Fabric 9
STONE FLOWER
Turquoise
GP173TQ

Fabric 10
ROW FLOWERS
Contrast
GP169CT

Fabric 11
SPOT
Silver
GP70SV

Fabric 12
ENCHANTED
Grey
GP172GY

Fabric 13
TIDDLYWINKS
Blue
GP171BL

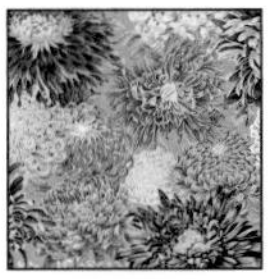

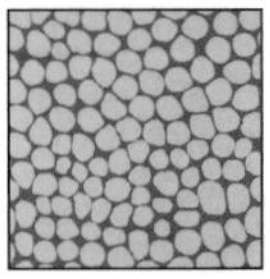

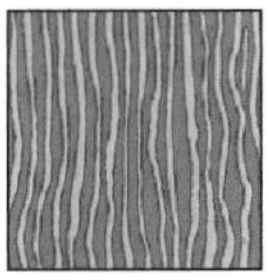

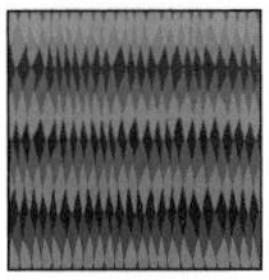

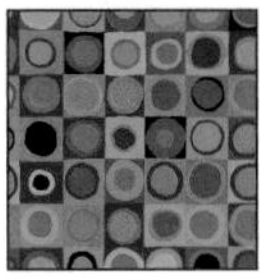

Backing and Binding Fabrics

Fabric 14
STONE FLOWER
Grey
QBGP005GY

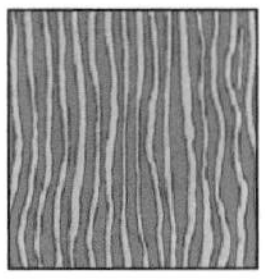

Fabric 4
CREASED
Turquoise
BM50TQ

CUTTING OUT
Cut fabrics from the width of the fabric and then sub-cut as described. Some of the fabrics are fussy cut.

Centre Panel
From Fabric 1 fussy cut a 12½in (31.8cm) square, centring on a large bloom of your choice.
From Fabric 2 cut 4 squares 3½in (9cm) for corner triangles.

Border 1
From Fabric 2 cut 2 strips 2in (5.1cm) wide across the width of the fabric. Sub-cut 2 strips 2in x 12½in (5.1cm x 31.8cm) and 2 strips 2in x 15½in (5.1cm x 39.4cm).

Border 2
From Fabric 2 cut 4 squares 3½in (9cm) for corner squares.
From Fabric 4 cut 24 squares 3½in (9cm).
From Fabric 5 cut 12 squares 3½in (9cm).
From Fabric 6 cut 16 squares 3½in (9cm).

Border 3
From Fabric 9 cut 4 strips 3½in x 27½in (9cm x 70cm).
From Fabric 2 cut 4 squares 3½in (9cm) for corner squares.

Border 4
From Fabric 7 cut 24 squares 3½in (9cm).
From Fabric 10 cut 24 squares 3½in (9cm).

Border 5
From Fabric 8 cut 112 squares 2⅜in (6cm). Cut each square diagonally once to make 2 triangles per square.
Total 224 triangles.
From Fabric 11 cut 56 squares 2⅝in (6.7cm).

Border 6
From Fabric 13 cut 5 strips 2in (5.1cm) wide across the width of the fabric. Fussy cut these strips to ensure the circles are straight. Join as necessary and then cut 2 strips 2in x 45½in (5.1cm x 115.6cm) and 2 strips 2in x 48½in (5.1cm x 123.2cm).

Border 7
From Fabric 12 cut 36 squares 4¾in (12cm).
From Fabric 3 cut 14 squares 7⅛in (18cm). Cut each square diagonally both ways to make 4 triangles per square.
Total 56 triangles.
From Fabric 3 cut 16 squares 3⅞in (9.8cm). Cut each square diagonally once to make 2 triangles per square.
Total 32 triangles.

Border 8
From Fabric 1 cut 3½in (9cm) strips across the width of the fabric. Each strip will give you 11 squares.
Cut 138 squares.
From Fabric 2 cut 3½in (9cm) strips across the width of the fabric.
Cut 138 squares.

Backing
From Fabric 14 cut a piece 86in x 86in (218.5cm x 218.5cm).

Binding
From binding Fabric 4 cut sufficient 2½in (6.4cm) strips diagonally across the fabric, which when joined will make a length of about 340in (8.6m). These

DIAGRAM 1

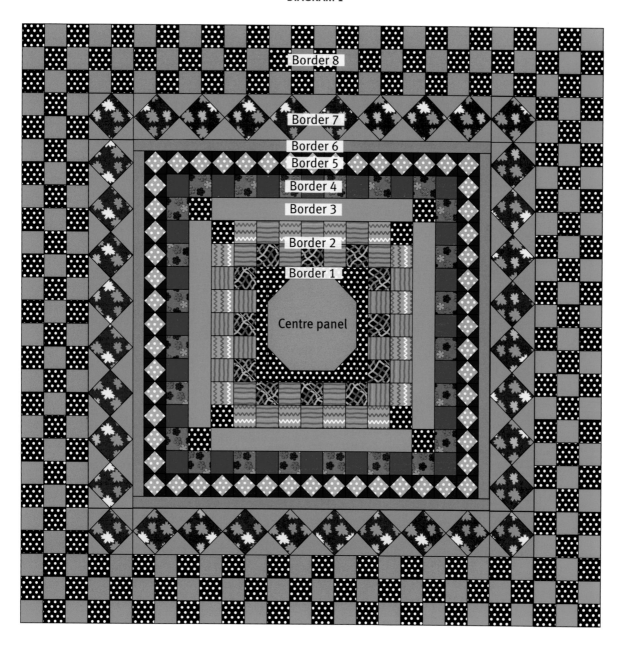

bias-cut strips will create an angled stripe pattern.

MAKING THE QUILT
Sew the centre panel and the borders of the quilt as described on pages 94 and 95 of Autumn Checkerboard, Making the Quilt. Follow Diagram 1 here for the colour placement and layout.

FINISHING THE QUILT
Finish the quilt as described on page 95 of Autumn Checkerboard.

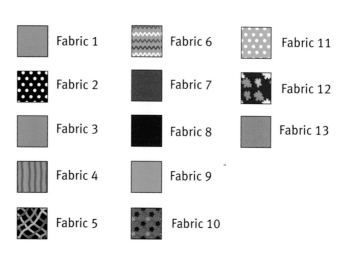

Fabric 1

Fabric 2

Fabric 3

Fabric 4

Fabric 5

Fabric 6

Fabric 7

Fabric 8

Fabric 9

Fabric 10

Fabric 11

Fabric 12

Fabric 13

jewel hexagons ***

Liza Prior Lucy

This delightful quilt has a centre of English paper-pieced hexagons joined into rings and appliquéd over fussy-cut squares of fabric. The rings are joined and appliquéd to a background panel and then surrounded by five borders. Borders 1 and 3 are unpieced, with corner squares. Border 2 is pieced with square-in-a-square blocks. Border 4 is pieced using checkerboard blocks set on point. Border 5 is unpieced, without corner squares.

TEMPLATES

84 hexagon papers with 1in (2.5cm) finished sides are needed. These can be purchased or cut from standard copier paper using the template provided on page 143. Please note that Template B is supplied with a ⅜in (1cm) seam allowance for English paper piecing.

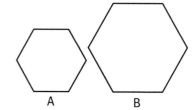

A   B

SIZE OF FINISHED QUILT
82in x 82in (208cm x 208cm)

FABRICS
Fabrics calculated at minimum width of 40in (102cm) and are cut across the width, unless otherwise stated. Fabrics have been given a number – see Fabric Swatch Diagram for details.

Patchwork Fabrics
PAPER FANS
Fabric 1	Black	2⅝yd (2.4m)

SHAGGY
Fabric 2	Black	1¾yd (1.6m)

LOTUS LEAF
Fabric 3	Purple	2½yd (2.3m)

SPOT
Fabric 4	Black	⅝yd (60cm)

PAPERWEIGHT
Fabric 5	Blue	1yd (90cm)
Fabric 6	Jewel	½yd (45cm)

JUMBLE
Fabric 7	Magenta	⅜yd (40cm)
Fabric 8	Orange	⅜yd (40cm)
Fabric 9	Blue	⅜yd (40cm)

ABORIGINAL DOT
Fabric 10	Charcoal	⅜yd (40cm)
Fabric 11	Plum	⅜yd (40cm)
Fabric 12	Leaf	⅜yd (40cm)
Fabric 13	Periwinkle	⅜yd (40cm)

Backing and Binding Fabrics
MILLEFIORE
Fabric 14	Blue	6½yd (6m)

ABORIGINAL DOT
Fabric 11	Plum	¾yd (70cm)

Batting
90in x 90in (228.5cm x 228.5cm)

Hexagon papers
84 hexagon papers 1in (2.5cm) finished side

FABRIC SWATCH DIAGRAM

Patchwork Fabrics

Fabric 1
PAPER FANS
Black
GP143BK

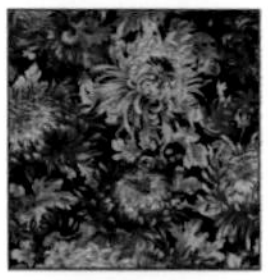

Fabric 2
SHAGGY
Black
PJ72BK

Fabric 3
LOTUS LEAF
Purple
GP29PU

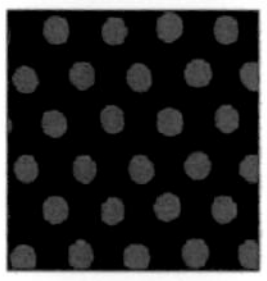

Fabric 4
SPOT
Black
GP70BK

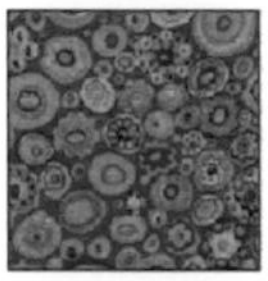

Fabric 5
PAPERWEIGHT
Blue
GP20BL

Fabric 6
PAPERWEIGHT
Jewel
GP20JL

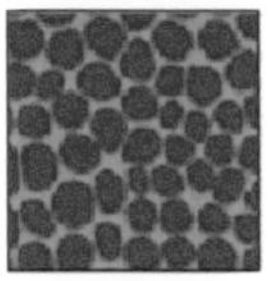

Fabric 7
JUMBLE
Magenta
BM53MG

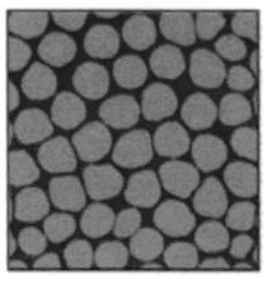

Fabric 8
JUMBLE
Orange
BM53OR

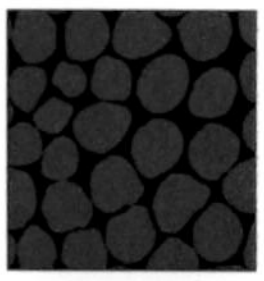

Fabric 9
JUMBLE
Blue
BM53BL

Fabric 10
ABORIGINAL DOT
Charcoal
GP71CC

Fabric 11
ABORIGINAL DOT
Plum
GP71PL

Fabric 12
ABORIGINAL DOT
Leaf
GP71LF

Fabric 13
ABORIGINAL DOT
Periwinkle
GP71PE

Backing and Binding Fabrics

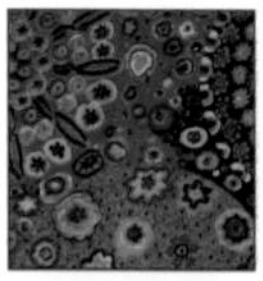

Fabric 14
MILLEFIORE
Blue
GP92BL

Fabric 11
ABORIGINAL DOT
Plum
GP71PL

CUTTING OUT

Please read the instructions carefully as some pieces are fussy cut.

Centre Panel

From Fabric 1 cut a 28in (71.1cm) square. This panel is oversized and will be trimmed later.

Using the smaller hexagon shape of Template A, cut 84 hexagons from paper. Using the larger hexagon shape of Template B (which includes a $\frac{3}{8}$in/1cm seam allowance for the fabric), cut 12 each from Fabric 7, Fabric 8, Fabric 9, Fabric 10, Fabric 11, Fabric 12 and Fabric 13. Total 84 fabric hexagons.

From Fabric 2 for the background squares, fussy cut 7 squares 6in (15.2cm), centring on the blossoms.

Border 1

From Fabric 6 cut 4 border strips each $3\frac{1}{4}$in x 27in (8.2cm x 68.6cm).
From Fabric 2 fussy cut 4 squares each $3\frac{1}{4}$in (8.2cm) for corner squares.

Border 5

Border 5 must be cut before Border 2 as it uses the *length* of the fabric. From Fabric 3 cut 2 lengths that match, each $5\frac{1}{2}$in x $82\frac{1}{2}$in (14cm x 209.5cm), and 2 lengths that match, each $5\frac{1}{2}$in x $72\frac{1}{2}$in (14cm x 184.2cm).

Border 2

From the remaining Fabric 3 cut *generous* $3\frac{3}{8}$in (8.6cm) strips across the remaining width and then cut into 36 squares.
From Fabric 4 cut $2\frac{7}{8}$in (7.3cm) strips across the width of the fabric. Cut into squares. Cut each square diagonally once to make two triangles per square. Each full width strip gives 26 triangles. Cut 144 triangles total.

Border 3

From Fabric 2 cut 4 border strips each $4\frac{1}{2}$in x $40\frac{1}{2}$in (11.4cm x 103cm).
From Fabric 6 cut 4 squares $4\frac{1}{2}$in (11.4cm).

Border 4

For the checkerboard blocks cut $2\frac{5}{8}$in (6.7cm) strips across the width of the fabric. Cut into squares. Each strip will give you 15 squares per full width.
Cut 160 squares from Fabric 5.

Cut 24 squares each from Fabric 7, Fabric 8, Fabric 9, Fabric 10, Fabric 11 and Fabric 12.
Cut 16 squares from Fabric 13. Total 320 squares.
For the setting triangles in this border use Fabric 1. This fabric is directional, so do *not* cut it doubled. Cut $6\frac{7}{8}$in (17.5cm) strips across the width of the fabric. Cut 40 squares $6\frac{7}{8}$in (17.5cm). Each strip will give you 5 squares per full width. With the fans facing up, cut 20 squares diagonally from top left to bottom right to form 40 triangles. Cut the other 20 squares diagonally the opposite way, from top right to bottom left to form 40 triangles. Total 80 triangles.

Backing

From Fabric 14 cut 2 pieces 40in x 90in (102cm x 228.6cm) and 2 pieces $45\frac{1}{2}$in x 11in (115.6cm x 28cm).

Binding

From binding Fabric 11 cut 9 strips $2\frac{1}{2}$in (6.4cm) x width of fabric. Sew together end to end.

MAKING THE QUILT

Use a $\frac{1}{4}$in (6mm) seam allowance throughout unless otherwise stated.

Centre Panel Making fabric hexagons

Follow the sequence in Diagram 1. Place a hexagon paper centrally on the wrong side of a fabric hexagon. Use a tiny dot of washable glue stick or a pin to hold them together. Fold the fabric tightly over the first side of the paper, finger press and baste into place. Continue folding and basting each side until the hexagon is complete.
Baste all the fabric hexagons to papers, 12 each from Fabric 7, Fabric 8, Fabric 9, Fabric 10, Fabric 11, Fabric 12 and Fabric 13.

Joining hexagons into rings Follow the

sequence shown in Diagram 2. Take 2 hexagons and place them right sides together, matching edges. Starting with a knotted thread slip the needle between the paper and the fabric and come out at the corner of the hexagon. Whipstitch through the very edge of the fabrics along one side, finishing with a double stitch to secure. Add the next hexagon and

continue like this until the ring is complete.
To remove the papers, use plenty of spray starch and press the rings on the back and front with the papers still in. Carefully remove the papers and press again. Handling the work very gently, baste the seam allowances into place around the inner and outer edge of the rings to keep the shape stable.
Lay a completed ring over a background square of Fabric 2 as shown in Diagram 2. Pin well and slipstitch into place around the inner ring. Trim excess fabric back to a $\frac{1}{4}$in (6mm) allowance.
Make 7 rings like this.

Assembling the hexagon rings Join the

7 rings together using whipstitch. The layout is shown in Diagram 3. Lay the joined rings centrally over the centre panel of Fabric 1, with the fans upright. Pin well and slipstitch the rings to the background around the outer edges and the gaps. The centre panel will eventually be trimmed, so be sure to stay within a $26\frac{1}{4}$in (66.7cm) square. To reduce bulk, snip into the fan fabric behind each ring and trim excess fabric to leave approx. $\frac{1}{4}$in (6mm) allowance. Trim the centre panel to 27in (68.6cm) square, keeping the hexagons central.

Border 1 Sew a border strip to each of

two opposite sides of the centre panel. Join a corner square to each end of the remaining 2 border strips and then add these to the top and bottom of the centre panel (see Diagram 4).

Border 2 Piece 36 square-in-a-square

blocks as shown in Diagram 5. Join blocks into 2 strips of 8 blocks and sew to the quilt sides. Join the remaining blocks into 2 strips of 10 blocks and sew to the quilt top and bottom, as shown in Diagram 4.

Border 3 Sew a border strip to two

opposite sides of the quilt. Sew a corner square to each end of the remaining 2 border strips and then sew these strips to the top and bottom of the quilt.

Border 4 Using the $2\frac{5}{8}$in (6.7cm)

squares, piece together 16-patch checkerboard blocks as shown in

DIAGRAM 1

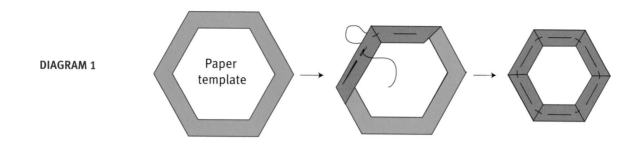

DIAGRAM 2

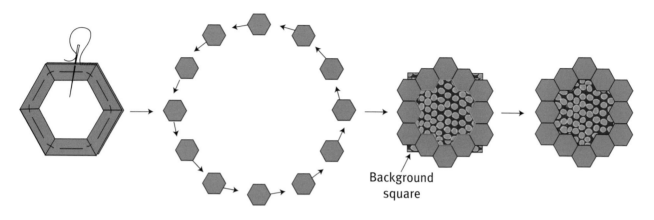

Background square

DIAGRAM 3

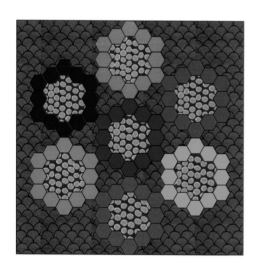

DIAGRAM 4

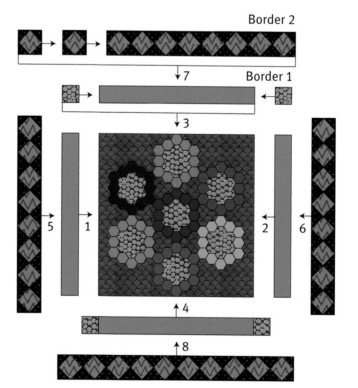

Border 2

Border 1

DIAGRAM 5

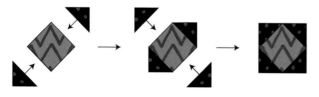

DIAGRAM 6

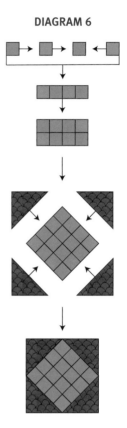

Diagram 6. Add setting triangles to each unit as shown. When positioning the triangles, keep the fan pattern upright. Join the blocks into 2 strips of 4 blocks and sew to the quilt sides. Join the remaining blocks into 2 strips of 6 blocks and sew to the quilt top and bottom, as shown in Diagram 7.

Border 5 Sew the shorter border strips to the sides of the quilt and then add the longer strips to the top and bottom to complete the quilt.

FINISHING THE QUILT
Press the quilt top. Using a ¼in (6mm) seam allowance, sew the two 45½in x 11in (115.6cm x 28cm) backing pieces together to make a long strip. Sew this piece between the wider pieces of backing to form a piece approx. 90in (228.5cm) square.
Layer the quilt top, batting and backing and baste together (see page 148).
Quilt as desired.
Trim the quilt edges and attach the binding (see page 149).

DIAGRAM 7

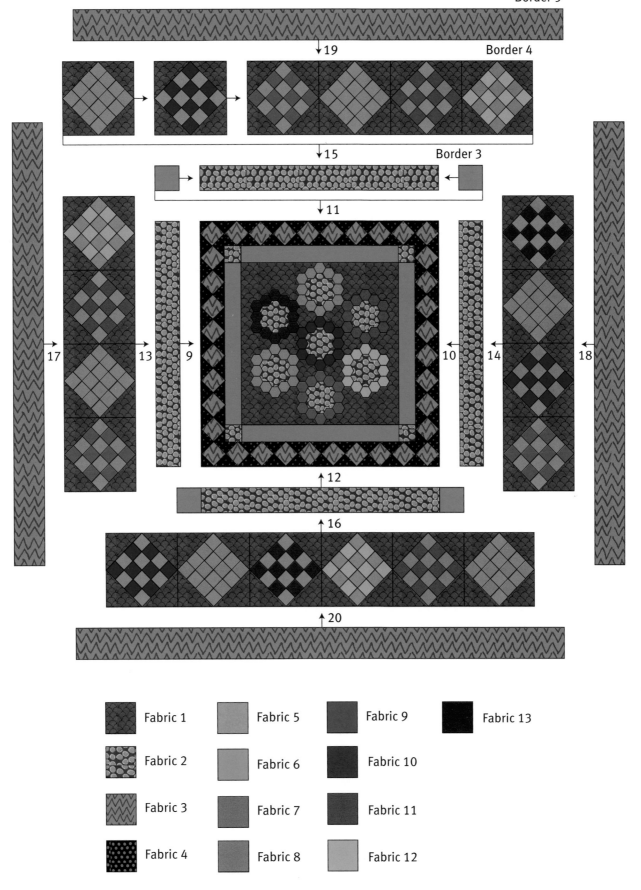

Border 5

Border 4

Border 3

Fabric 1	Fabric 5	Fabric 9
Fabric 2	Fabric 6	Fabric 10
Fabric 3	Fabric 7	Fabric 11
Fabric 4	Fabric 8	Fabric 12

Fabric 13

folded ribbons ***

Kaffe Fassett

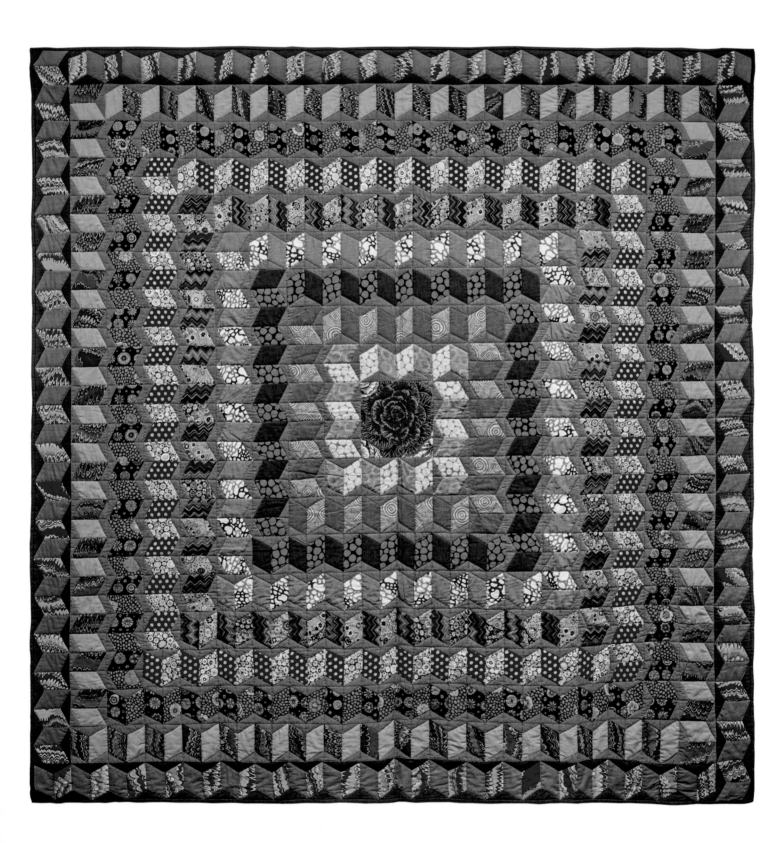

On a visit to my house, Liza noticed a doodle of mine on my studio table and thought it might have potential for a quilt. After many hours on the Electric Quilt design software, she figured out how to design and orient the blocks in a logical manner. She then asked me to colour the graphic, and the result is this original medallion quilt. It is not hard to do, but it is a bit time-consuming.

SIZE OF FINISHED QUILT
80in x 80in (203cm x 203cm)

FABRICS
Fabrics calculated at minimum width of 40in (102cm) and are cut across the width, unless otherwise stated. Fabrics have been given a number – see Fabric Swatch Diagram overleaf for details.

Patchwork Fabrics
BRASSICA

Fabric 1	Dark	½yd (45cm)

SHOT COTTON

Fabric 2	Smoky	3¼yd (3m)
Fabric 3	Eucalyptus	¼yd (25cm)
Fabric 4	Thunder	1yd (90cm)
Fabric 5	Spruce	⅜yd (40cm)
Fabric 6	Galvanized	⅝yd (60cm)
Fabric 7	Pewter	⅝yd (60cm)

JUMBLE

Fabric 8	Moss	¼yd (25cm)
Fabric 9	Animal	¼yd (25cm)

ABORIGINAL DOT

Fabric 10	Forest	¼yd (25cm)

MILLEFIORE

Fabric 11	Antique	⅜yd (40cm)

ZIG ZAG

Fabric 12	Black	⅜yd (40cm)

PAPERWEIGHT

Fabric 13	Algae	½yd (45cm)

SPOT

Fabric 14	Eggplant	½yd (45cm)

GUINEA FLOWER

Fabric 15	Brown	½yd (45cm)

WHIRLIGIG

Fabric 16	Black	½yd (45cm)

GOOD VIBRATIONS

Fabric 17	Orange	¼yd (25cm)

END PAPERS

Fabric 18	Moss	⅝yd (60cm)
Fabric 19	Purple	⅝yd (60cm)

MOSS

Fabric 20	Green	⅜yd (40cm)

Backing and Binding Fabrics
MILLEFIORE

Fabric 21	Dark	6yd (5.4m)

SHOT COTTON

Fabric 4	Thunder	¾yd (70cm)

Batting
88in x 88in (223.5cm x 223.5cm)

TEMPLATES

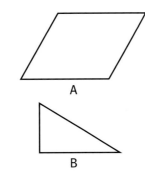

CUTTING OUT
All fabric is cut from strips selvedge to selvedge.
The centre of the quilt is an 8½in (21.6cm) square of Fabric 1. Find the cabbage that you favour and adjust how much fabric you buy accordingly.
Do not cut the printed fabrics double as the shapes are not reversible. You can cut the Shot Cottons double as they do not have a right or wrong side and can be flipped over. We recommend using Mary Ellen's Best Press or starch on the Shot Cottons before cutting.

Centre Square
From Fabric 1 fussy cut an 8½in (21.6cm) square.

Template A Shapes
Remember not to cut Template A with the printed fabric doubled, as the shape is not reversible. Each 'round' has a light colour and a dark colour. For all the *dark* print fabrics, place Template A *right side up* on the front side of the fabric and cut.

For all the *light* print fabrics, place the template *wrong side up* on the front side of the fabric. Cut strips 2½in (6.4cm) across the width of the fabric. Each 2½in (6.4cm) strip will give 11 parallelograms. From dark fabrics cut the following number of parallelograms. Keep the darks together:
Fabric 10 cut 12; Fabric 3 cut 20; Fabric 4 cut 28; Fabric 5 cut 36; Fabric 12 cut 44; Fabric 14 cut 52; Fabric 16 cut 60; Fabric 18 cut 68; Fabric 7 cut 76.
From light fabrics cut the following number of parallelograms. Keep the lights together:
Fabric 8 cut 12; Fabric 17 cut 20; Fabric 9 cut 28; Fabric 20 cut 36; Fabric 11 cut 44; Fabric 13 cut 52; Fabric 15 cut 60; Fabric 6 cut 68; Fabric 19 cut 76.

Template B Shapes
To cut these triangles, use Template B on page 141. Alternatively, if you don't want to use the template, cut a rectangle 3⅛in (8cm) wide x 1⅞in (4.8cm) tall and then cut it once along the diagonal to give two triangles from each rectangle. Ensure the fabric grain runs along the length of the triangle, as in Diagram 1.
Note: If you plan to use a print fabric rather than a solid, then you will definitely need to use the template. It will also need to be used in reverse for half of the pieces.
From Fabric 2 cut 54 strips 1⅞in (4.8cm) across the width of the fabric. Using Template B, cut 1,280 triangles by flipping the template back and forth. Each strip will give 24 triangles.
From Fabric 4 cut 13 strips 1⅞in (4.8cm) across the width of the fabric. Using Template B, cut 304 triangles by flipping the template back and forth.

Backing
From Fabric 21, cut two panels 90in (228.6cm) long and cut the remaining fabric lengthwise into three 10in (25.4cm) wide lengths.

DIAGRAM 1

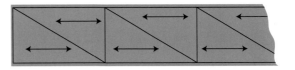

Patchwork Fabrics

Fabric 1
BRASSICA
Dark
PJ51DK

Fabric 12
ZIG ZAG
Black
BM43BK

Fabric 2
SHOT COTTON
Smoky
SC20SM

Fabric 13
PAPERWEIGHT
Algae
GP20AL

Fabric 3
SHOT COTTON
Eucalyptus
SC90EU

Fabric 14
SPOT
Eggplant
GP70EG

Fabric 4
SHOT COTTON
Thunder
SC06TH

Fabric 15
GUINEA FLOWER
Brown
GP59BR

Fabric 5
SHOT COTTON
Spruce
SC89SC

Fabric 16
WHIRLIGIG
Black
GP166BK

Fabric 6
SHOT COTTON
Galvanized
SC87GA

Fabric 17
GOOD VIBRATIONS
Orange
BM65OR

Fabric 7
SHOT COTTON
Pewter
SC22PW

Fabric 18
END PAPERS
Moss
GP159MS

Fabric 8
JUMBLE
Moss
BM53MS

Fabric 19
END PAPERS
Purple
GP159PU

Fabric 9
JUMBLE
Animal
BM53AM

Fabric 20
MOSS
Green
BM68GN

Fabric 10
ABORIGINAL DOT
Forest
GP71FO

Backing and Binding Fabrics

Fabric 21
MILLEFIORE
Dark
GP92DK

Fabric 11
MILLEFIORE
Antique
GP92AN

Fabric 4
SHOT COTTON
Thunder
SC06TH

Binding

From binding Fabric 4 cut nine 2½in (6.4cm) wide strips across the width of the fabric. Sew together end to end.

MAKING THE BLOCKS

Each block has one light A parallelogram, one dark A parallelogram and 4 Shot Cotton B triangles.

For Borders 1 to 8, use Fabric 2 for the B triangles. For Border 9, use Fabric 4 for the B triangles.

Following Diagram 2, sew a B triangle to the top and bottom of a light A parallelogram, offsetting the triangles as shown, and press. Repeat with a dark A parallelogram and two B triangles. Now sew the two sides of the block together as in Diagram 3. Make all of the blocks the same way, but changing the colours

of the A parallelograms in each border, as shown in Diagram 4 and Diagram 5 on page 110.

Make the following numbers of blocks for the borders:

Border 1 make 12 blocks; Border 2 make 20 blocks; Border 3 make 28 blocks; Border 4 make 36 blocks; Border 5 make 44 blocks; Border 6 make 52 blocks; Border 7 make 60 blocks; Border 8 make 68 blocks; Border 9 make 76 blocks.

ASSEMBLING THE QUILT

Start with the centre square and follow Diagram 4 to sew the blocks together for Border 1. Add pairs of blocks to the top and bottom of the centre square, and then sew rows of 4 blocks together on the sides. It is important to arrange each block the correct way as you sew, to maintain the

folded ribbon pattern of light and dark. Now change block colour and add Border 2 in the same way. Continue like this, working outwards and following Diagram 5 carefully.

FINISHING THE QUILT

Press the quilt top. Remove selvedges and sew the 3 narrow pieces of backing fabric end to end, trimmed to 90in (228.6cm). Sew the narrow strip between the two wider panels using a ¼in (6mm) seam allowance to form a piece approx. 90in (228.6cm) square.

Layer the quilt top, batting and backing and baste together (see page 148).

Quilt as desired.

Trim the quilt edges and attach the binding (see page 149).

DIAGRAM 2

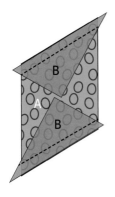

DIAGRAM 3

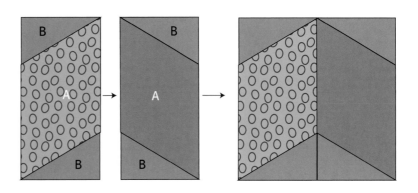

DIAGRAM 4

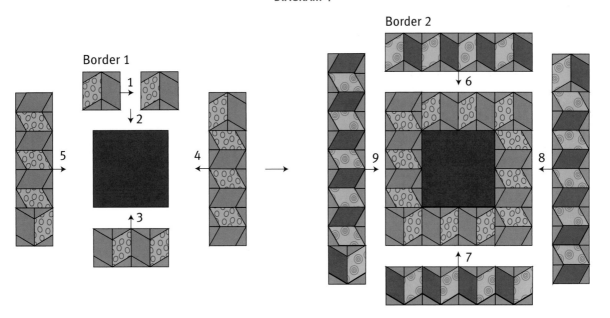

DIAGRAM 5

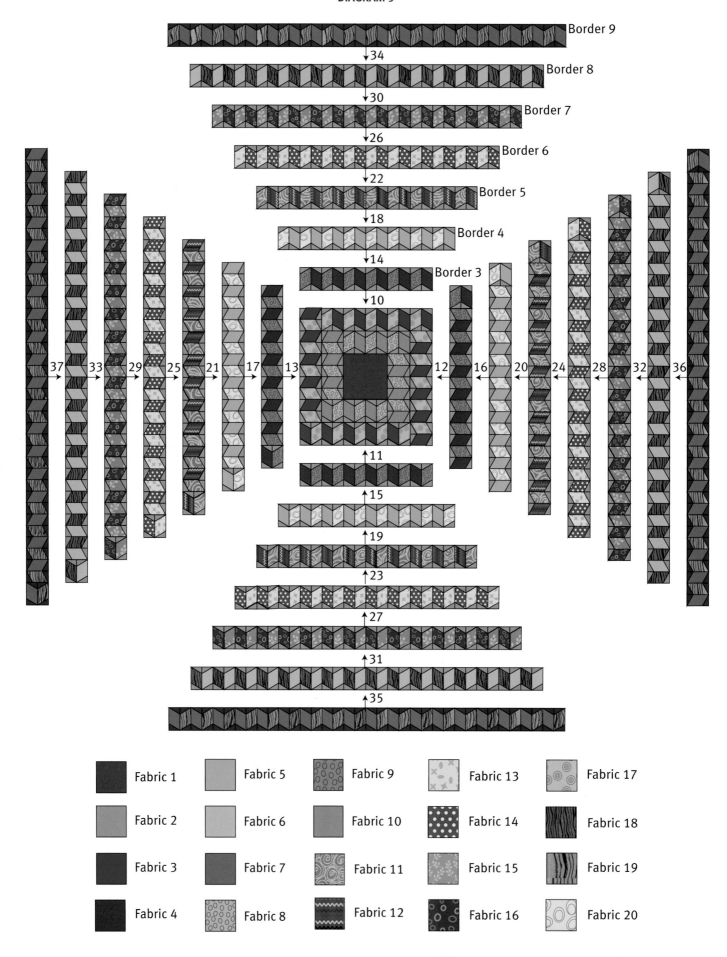

Border 9

Border 8

Border 7

Border 6

Border 5

Border 4

Border 3

	Fabric 1		Fabric 5		Fabric 9		Fabric 13		Fabric 17
	Fabric 2		Fabric 6		Fabric 10		Fabric 14		Fabric 18
	Fabric 3		Fabric 7		Fabric 11		Fabric 15		Fabric 19
	Fabric 4		Fabric 8		Fabric 12		Fabric 16		Fabric 20

cool imari plate ***

Corienne Kramer

This quilt has an appliquéd Imari plate in the centre and works outwards through nine borders, alternating unpieced with pieced, to create a beautiful but challenging design.

SIZE OF FINISHED QUILT
89in x 89in (226cm x 226cm)

FABRICS
Fabrics calculated at minimum width of 40in (102cm) and are cut across the width, unless otherwise stated. Fabrics have been given a number – see Fabric Swatch Diagram for details.

Patchwork Fabrics
MILLEFIORE
Fabric 1	Lilac	¾yd (70cm)
Fabric 2	Pink	½yd (45cm)
Fabric 3	Aqua	½yd (45cm)
Fabric 4	Jade	½yd (45cm)

PAPERWEIGHT
| Fabric 5 | Blue | ½yd (45cm) |
| Fabric 6 | Sludge | ⅞yd (80cm) |

COLEUS
| Fabric 7 | Lavender | 1¼yd (1.2m) |

GOOD VIBRATIONS
| Fabric 8 | Pink | ½yd (45cm) |
| Fabric 9 | Orange | ⅛yd (15cm) |

JUPITER
| Fabric 10 | Jade | ½yd (45cm) |

MAD PLAID
| Fabric 11 | Turquoise | 1yd (90cm) |

SPOT
Fabric 12	Lavender	½yd (45cm)
Fabric 13	Hydrangea	½yd (45cm)
Fabric 14	Sapphire	⅝yd (60cm)
Fabric 15	Green	⅜yd (40cm)

LOTUS LEAF
| Fabric 16 | Purple | ⅝yd (60cm) |

BRASSICA
| Fabric 17 | Dark | ½yd (45cm) |

DREAM
| Fabric 18 | Purple | ⅝yd (60cm) |

JUMBLE
| Fabric 19 | Turquoise | ¾yd (70cm) |

Backing and Binding Fabrics
BRASSICA
| Fabric 20 | Green | 7⅛yd (6.5m) |

PAPERWEIGHT
| Fabric 5 | Blue | ¾yd (70cm) |

Batting
98in x 98in (249cm x 249cm)

FABRIC SWATCH DIAGRAM

Patchwork Fabrics

Fabric 1
MILLEFIORE
Lilac
GP92LI

Fabric 2
MILLEFIORE
Pink
GP92PK

Fabric 3
MILLEFIORE
Aqua
GP92AQ

Fabric 4
MILLEFIORE
Jade
GP92JA

Fabric 5
PAPERWEIGHT
Blue
GP20BL

Fabric 6
PAPERWEIGHT
Sludge
GP20SL

Fabric 7
COLEUS
Lavender
PJ30LV

Fabric 8
GOOD VIBRATIONS
Pink
BM65PK

Fabric 9
GOOD VIBRATIONS
Orange
BM65OR

Fabric 10
JUPITER
Jade
GP131JA

Fabric 11
MAD PLAID
Turquoise
BM37TQ

Fabric 12
SPOT
Lavender
GP70LV

Fabric 13
SPOT
Hydrangea
GP70HY

Fabric 14
SPOT
Sapphire
GP70SP

Fabric 15
SPOT
Green
GP70GN

Fabric 16
LOTUS LEAF
Purple
GP29PU

Fabric 17
BRASSICA
Dark
PJ51DK

Fabric 18
DREAM
Purple
GP148PU

Fabric 19
JUMBLE
Turquoise
BM53TQ

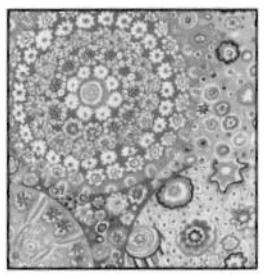

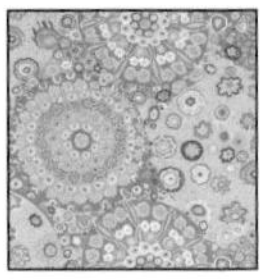

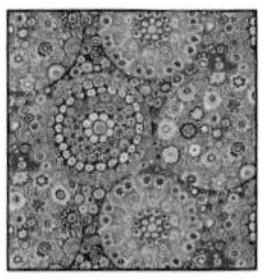

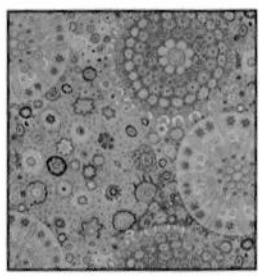

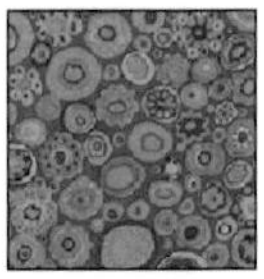

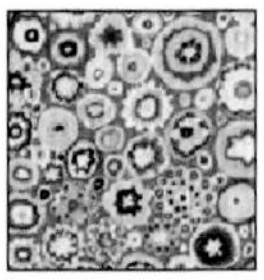

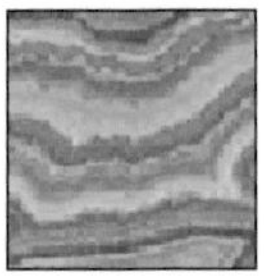

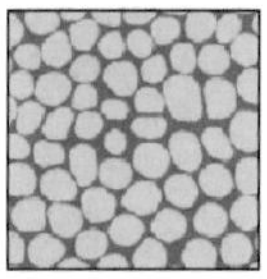

Backing and Binding Fabrics

Fabric 20
BRASSICA
Green
PJ51GN

Fabric 5
PAPERWEIGHT
Blue
GP20BL

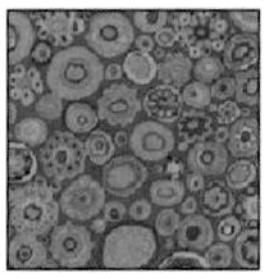

TEMPLATES

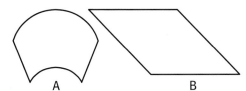

A   B

CUTTING OUT

Some of the pieces need to be cut with *scant* measurements, which means cutting them 1/16in (2mm) smaller than the measurement quoted. Other pieces need *generous* measurements, which means cutting them 1/16in (2mm) larger than the measurement quoted. To gauge these measurements, use the space *between* the 1/8in marks on your rotary ruler.

Centre Appliqué Panel

From Fabric 1 cut a square 14in (35.5cm) for the appliqué background. This is oversize and will be trimmed when the hand appliqué is complete.

For the appliqué shapes, please note that the templates do not include a seam allowance, to allow you to use the appliqué method you prefer. If using turned-edge appliqué add a 1/4in–3/8in (6mm–1cm) seam allowance all round. If using raw-edge fused appliqué, no seam allowance is needed at all; simply fuse the fusible web to the back of the fabrics before cutting out.

From Fabric 2 cut a circle 8½in (21.6cm) diameter (includes seam allowance).

From Fabric 5, and using Template A, cut 4 petals (add seam allowance if needed).

From Fabric 7, and using Template A, cut 4 petals (add seam allowance if needed).

Border 1

From Fabric 8 cut 2 strips 1½in (3.8cm) wide across the width of the fabric. From these cut 2 strips 1½in x 13½in (3.8cm x 34.3cm) for the sides of the quilt and 2 strips 1½in x 15½in (3.8cm x 39.4cm) for the top and bottom.

Border 2

From Fabric 6 cut 32 squares 3⅜in (8.6cm) and cut once diagonally, making two triangles from each square. Total 64 triangles.

From Fabric 9 cut 16 squares a *scant* 1¾in (4.4cm).

From Fabric 10 cut 32 rectangles a *scant* 1¾in (4.4cm) x a *generous* 4in (10.2cm), ensuring that the fabric stripes run across the length.

From Fabric 10 cut 32 squares a *scant* 1¾in (4.4cm).

Border 3

From Fabric 11 cut 4 strips 2in (5.1cm) wide across the width of the fabric. From these cut 2 strips 2in x 25½in (5.1cm x 64.8cm) for the sides and 2 strips 2in x 28½in (5.1cm x 72.4cm) for the top and bottom.

Border 4

Cut 4⅞in (12.4cm) squares and cut each square once diagonally, making two triangles from each square. Total 64 triangles. Cut the following number of squares from each fabric: Fabric 1 cut 6 squares (12 triangles); Fabric 2 cut 4 (8 triangles); Fabric 3 cut 1 (2 triangles); Fabric 5 cut 2 (4 triangles, only 3 needed); Fabric 7 cut 3 (6 triangles); Fabric 8 cut 3 (6 triangles); Fabric 12 cut 3 (6 triangles); Fabric 13 cut 3 (6 triangles); Fabric 16 cut 3 (6 triangles); Fabric 17 cut 1 (2 triangles); Fabric 18 cut 4 (8 triangles, only 7 needed).

Border 5

From Fabric 19 cut 4 strips 3½in (9cm) across the width of the fabric. Join as necessary and cut 2 strips 3½in x 36½in (9cm x 92.7cm) for the sides and 2 strips 3½in x 42½in (9cm x 108cm) for the top and bottom.

Border 6

Block centres Cut *scant* 5¾in (14.6cm) strips across the width of the fabric. Each strip will give you 7 squares per full width. Total 28 squares. Cut the following number of squares from each fabric: Fabric 3 cut 3; Fabric 7 cut 4; Fabric 16 cut 7; Fabric 17 cut 7 and Fabric 18 cut 7.

Block corner triangles Cut squares 4⅜in (11.1cm) and cut each square once diagonally, making two triangles from each square. Cut the following number of squares from each fabric: Fabric 4 cut 14 squares (for 28 triangles); Fabric 14 cut 28 squares (for 56 triangles); Fabric 15 cut 14 squares (for 28 triangles).

Border 7

From Fabric 3 cut 8 strips 2¾in (7cm) wide across the width of the fabric. Join as necessary and then cut 2 strips 2¾in x 56½in (7cm x 143.5cm) for the sides and 2 strips 2¾in x 61in (7cm x 155cm) for the top and bottom.

Border 8

Each star block needs one background fabric and two different fabrics for the star points. A different fabric is used for the sashing between the blocks. Diagram 6 shows the fabrics used and their positions.

Sashing From Fabric 11 cut 20 rectangles 3in x 12½in (7.6cm x 31.8cm).

Star block backgrounds Each star has 4 background squares and 8 background triangles (one set). Cut the background squares 4in (10.2cm). Cut the background triangles from squares 3⅜in (8.6cm). Cut each 3⅜in (8.6cm) square once diagonally, making two triangles from each square.

From Fabric 1 cut 6 sets (24 squares, 48 triangles).

From Fabric 2 cut 4 sets (16 squares, 32 triangles).

From Fabric 6 cut 4 sets (16 squares, 32 triangles).

From Fabric 12 cut 3 sets (12 squares, 24 triangles).

From Fabric 13 cut 3 sets (12 squares, 24 triangles).

Star block star points Cut the star points using Template B. For each star you need a set of 4 matching parallelograms from one fabric and a set of 4 matching from another – this makes up one set. A total of 160 parallelograms are needed. Cut the fabric strips 3in (7.6cm) deep across the fabric width. You will get 8 shapes from a strip.

From Fabric 3 cut 1 set (4 B).

From Fabric 4 cut 2 sets (8 B).

From Fabric 5 cut 3 sets (12 B).

From Fabric 6 cut 3 sets (12 B).

From Fabric 7 cut 5 sets (20 B).

From Fabric 8 cut 3 sets (12 B).

From Fabric 10 cut 4 sets (16 B).

From Fabric 12 cut 2 sets (8 B).

From Fabric 16 cut 5 sets (20 B).

From Fabric 17 cut 4 sets (16 B).

From Fabric 18 cut 5 sets (20 B).

From Fabric 19 cut 3 sets (12 B).

Border 9

From Fabric 7 cut 9 strips 2¾in (7cm) across the width of the fabric. Join as necessary and cut 2 strips 2¾in x 85in (7cm x 216cm) for the sides and 2 strips 2¾in x 89½in (7cm x 227.3cm) for the top and bottom.

Backing

From Fabric 20 cut 2 pieces 40in x 98in (102cm x 249cm). Cut the remaining yardage into 2 strips 19in x 50in (48.3cm x 127cm).

Binding

From binding Fabric 5 cut 10 strips 2½in (6.4cm) across the width of the fabric. Sew togther end to end.

MAKING THE QUILT

The assembly of each border is described, with reference to the relevant diagrams. For each border, add the side strips first and then the top and bottom, pressing after every seam.

Centre appliqué panel Using your preferred method of appliqué, stitch the petals together to form a ring as shown in Diagram 1a and press. Carefully place the ring on the circle of Fabric 2 and stitch the inner edge of the petals to the circle. Centre the complete ring on the large square of Fabric 1 and appliqué into place (Diagram 1b). Trim the centre panel to 13½in (34.3cm) square.

Border 1 Sew the shorter strips to the sides of the centre panel. Sew the longer strips to the top and bottom.

Border 2 The blocks for this border are all made the same way and with the same fabrics. Follow Diagram 2 (a to d) for the piecing of a block. Make 16 blocks in total. Each unfinished block should be 5½in (14cm) square. Sew 2 strips of 3 blocks together and sew to the sides of the quilt. Sew 2 strips of 5 blocks together and sew to the top and bottom.

Border 3 Sew the shorter strips to the sides of the centre panel. Sew the longer strips to the top and bottom.

Border 4 Match the triangles into dark/ light pairs – you can choose your own combinations or follow the order shown in Diagram 5. Sew each pair together to make 32 half-square triangle blocks. Each unfinished block should be 4½in (11.4cm) square.
Sew 2 strips of 7 blocks together and sew to the sides of the quilt. Sew 2 strips of 9 blocks together and sew to the top and bottom.

Border 5 Sew the shorter strips to the sides of the centre panel. Sew the longer strips to the top and bottom.

Border 6 The blocks for this border are all made in the same way. The squares on point are placed randomly (or follow the order in Diagram 5 on page 110). The blocks use triangles of Fabric 14 and Fabric 15 for one block colourway, and triangles of Fabric 14 and Fabric 4 for the other colourway. Follow Diagram 3 for the piecing of a block. Make 28 blocks in total. Each unfinished block should be 7½in (19cm) square.
Sew 2 strips of 6 blocks together, arranging the blocks so the Fabric 14 triangles all face the same direction, and sew to the sides of the quilt. Sew 2 strips of 8 blocks together in the same way and sew to the top and bottom.

Border 7 Sew the shorter strips to the sides of the centre panel. Sew the longer strips to the top and bottom.

Border 8 The eight-point star blocks for this border are all made in the same way. Follow Diagram 4 (a to c) for the piecing of a block. Note that set-in (Y) seams are needed for some parts of the block assembly. Follow the fabric positions shown in Diagram 6 on page 111. Make 20 blocks in total. Each unfinished block should be 12½in (31.8cm) square.
Sew 2 strips of 4 blocks together, with a sashing strip between the blocks and at both ends of the row. Sew to the sides of the quilt. Sew 2 strips of 6 blocks together, with a sashing strip between the blocks. Sew to the top and bottom of the quilt.

DIAGRAM 1

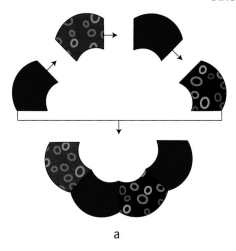

a

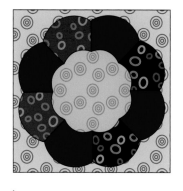

b

DIAGRAM 2

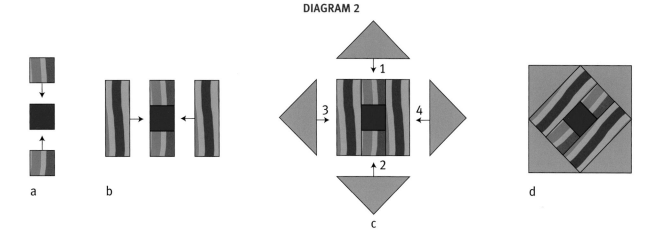

a   b   c   d

DIAGRAM 3

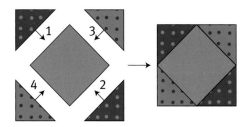

DIAGRAM 4

a

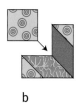

b

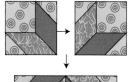

c

Border 9 Sew the shorter strips to the sides of the centre panel. Sew the longer strips to the top and bottom of the quilt to finish.

FINISHING THE QUILT
Press the quilt top. Sew the 2 narrow backing pieces 19in x 50in (48.3cm x 127cm) together into a long strip and trim to 98in (249cm). Sew this narrow strip between the two wider pieces to form a piece 98in (249cm) square.
Layer the quilt top, batting and backing and baste together (see page 148).
Quilt as desired.
Trim the quilt edges and attach the binding (see page 149).

DIAGRAM 5

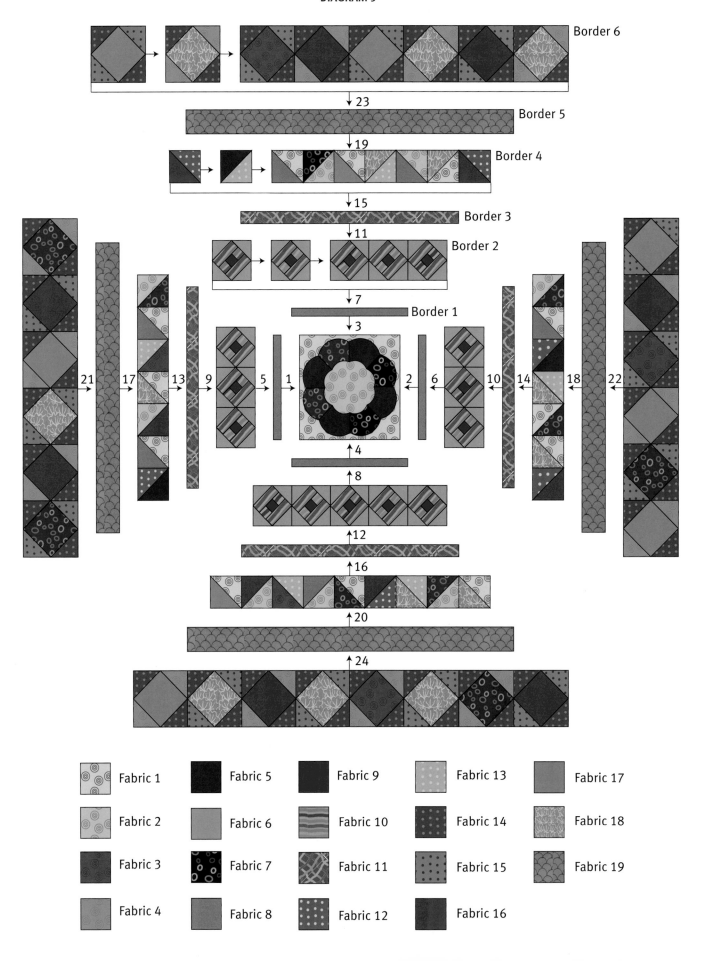

Border 6

Border 5

Border 4

Border 3

Border 2

Border 1

Fabric 1
Fabric 2
Fabric 3
Fabric 4
Fabric 5
Fabric 6
Fabric 7
Fabric 8
Fabric 9
Fabric 10
Fabric 11
Fabric 12
Fabric 13
Fabric 14
Fabric 15
Fabric 16
Fabric 17
Fabric 18
Fabric 19

DIAGRAM 6

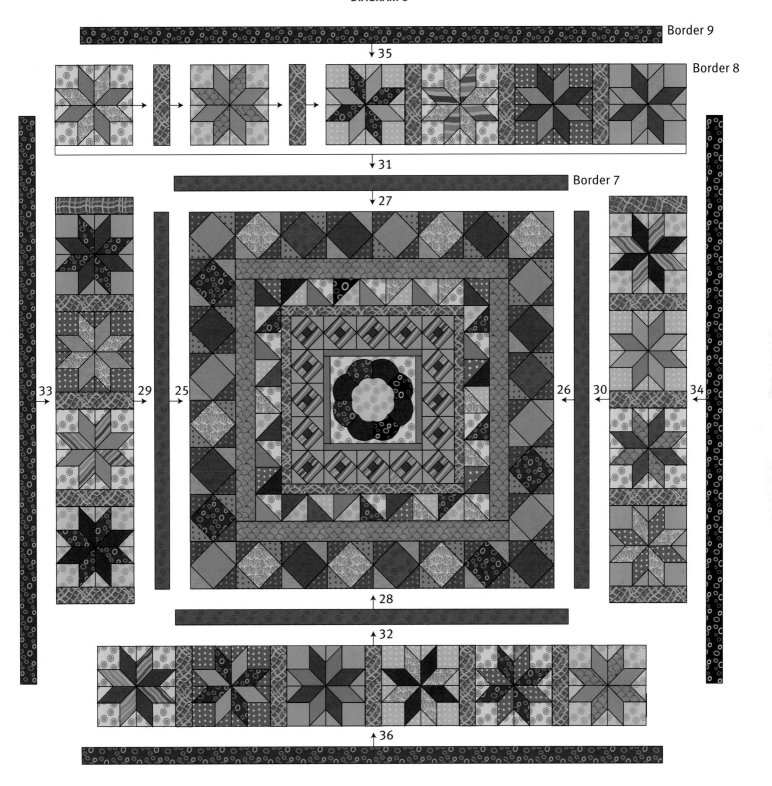

Border 9

Border 8

35

31

Border 7

27

33 29 25 26 30 34

28

32

36

golden medallion ***

Liza Prior Lucy

This quilt has a central panel where the pieced squares are arranged on point to create a focal point. Alternating pieced and unpieced borders surround this, with the triangles in the second border fussy cut to showcase a flower motif in each.

SIZE OF FINISHED QUILT
96in x (244cm x 244cm)

FABRICS
Fabrics calculated at minimum width of 40in (102cm) and are cut across the width, unless otherwise stated. Fabrics have been given a number – see Fabric Swatch Diagram for details.

Patchwork Fabrics
ROMAN GLASS
| Fabric 1 | Gold | ¾yd (70cm) |
ABORIGINAL DOT
Fabric 2	Purple	⅛yd (15cm)
Fabric 3	Lime	⅛yd (15cm)
Fabric 4	Wisteria	⅛yd (15cm)
SPOT
Fabric 5	Tobacco	¼yd (25cm)
Fabric 6	Storm	⅛yd (15cm)
Fabric 7	Apple	⅛yd (15cm)
Fabric 8	Duck Egg	⅛yd (15cm)
Fabric 9	Melon	⅛yd (15cm)
JUMBLE
Fabric 10	Moss	1½yd (1.4m)
PAPERWEIGHT
Fabric 11	Sludge	⅛yd (15cm)
Fabric 12	Pumpkin	¼yd (25cm)
BAROQUE FLORAL
Fabric 13	Brown	2yd (1.8m)
GUINEA FLOWER
Fabric 14	Green	1yd (90cm)
POPPY GARDEN
Fabric 15	Orange	1½yd (1.4cm)
JUPITER
Fabric 16	Brown	1⅜yd (1.25cm)
BRASSICA
Fabric 17	Orange	2¾yd (2.5m)

Backing and Binding Fabrics
FRUIT MANDALA
| Fabric 18 | Red | 3yd (2.75m) |
of extra-wide fabric (108in/274cm)
JUPITER
| Fabric 16 | Brown | ¾yd (70cm) |

Batting
104in x 104in (264cm x 264cm)

FABRIC SWATCH DIAGRAM

Patchwork Fabrics

Fabric 1
ROMAN GLASS
Gold
GP01GD

Fabric 2
ABORIGINAL DOT
Purple
GP71PU

Fabric 3
ABORIGINAL DOT
Lime
GP71LM

Fabric 4
ABORIGINAL DOT
Wisteria
GP71WS

Fabric 5
SPOT
Tobacco
GP70TO

Fabric 6
SPOT
Storm
GP70ST

Fabric 7
SPOT
Apple
GP70AL

Fabric 8
SPOT
Duck Egg
GP70DE

Fabric 9
SPOT
Melon
GP70ME

Fabric 10
JUMBLE
Moss
BM53MS

Fabric 11
PAPERWEIGHT
Sludge
GP20SL

Fabric 12
PAPERWEIGHT
Pumpkin
GP20PN

Fabric 13
BAROQUE FLORAL
Brown
PJ90BR

Fabric 14
GUINEA FLOWER
Green
GP59GN

Fabric 15
POPPY GARDEN
Orange
PJ95OR

Fabric 16
JUPITER
Brown
GP131BR

Fabric 17
BRASSICA
Orange
PJ51OR

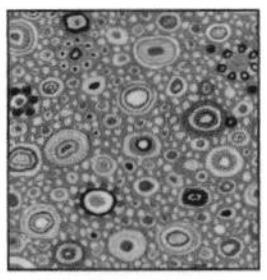

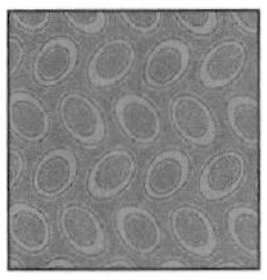

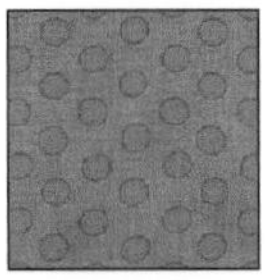

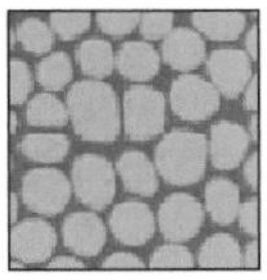

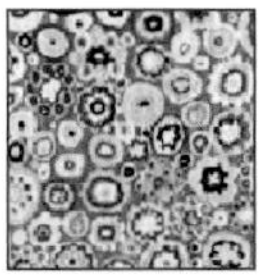

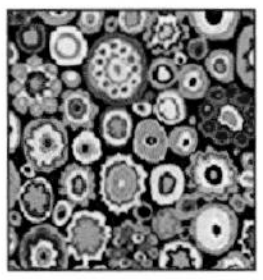

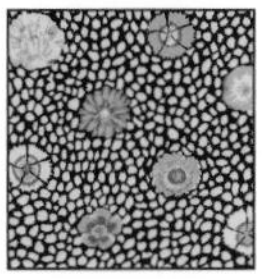

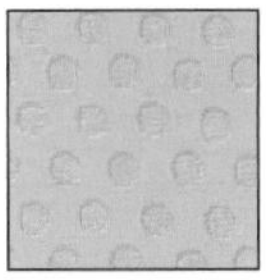

Backing and Binding Fabrics

Fabric 18
FRUIT MANDALA
Red
QBGP003RD

Fabric 16
JUPITER
Brown
GP131BR

TEMPLATES

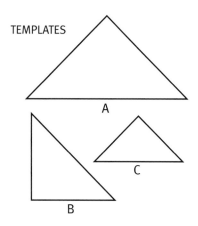

A

C

B

Note that half of Template A is provided. Create the full template by drawing it on folded paper, as described on page XX. Pay attention to the grainline arrows on the templates.

CUTTING OUT
Centre Panel
For the on-point centre, cut 2½in (6.4cm) squares in the following fabrics and quantities: Fabric 1 cut 144; Fabric 2 cut 10; Fabric 3 cut 11; Fabric 4 cut 14; Fabric 5 cut 18; Fabric 6 cut 13; Fabric 7 cut 11; Fabric 8 cut 7; Fabric 9 cut 9; Fabric 10 cut 27; Fabric 11 cut 7; Fabric 12 cut 18. Total 289 squares.
For the large triangles, from Fabric 13 cut 2 squares 24⅞in (63.2cm). Cut each square once diagonally, making 4 triangles in total.

Border 1
From Fabric 15, and using Template A, fussy cut 12 single blossoms.
Note: It may not be possible to contain a complete flower within each triangle, which is fine. There is enough yardage to select different blossoms, so pick your favourites.
From Fabric 15 and using Template B cut 8 triangles (not fussy cut).
From Fabric 14 cut 4 strips 6⅝in (16.8cm) across the width of the fabric. Using Template A cut 16 triangles.
From Fabric 14 cut 4 squares 6½in (16.5cm) for corner squares.

Border 2
From Fabric 16 cut 7 strips 6½in (16.5cm) across the width of the fabric. Sew together end to end and then cut 2 lengths 72½in (184.2cm) and 2 lengths 60½in (153.7cm).

Border 3
From Fabric 13 cut 52 squares 4¾in (12cm).
From Fabric 10 cut 10 strips 3⅝in (9.2cm) wide across the width of the fabric. Using Template C, place the long side of the template parallel to the long edge of the fabric and flip back and forth to cut 9 triangles from each strip. Total 88 triangles.
From Fabric 10 cut 16 squares 3⅞in (9.8cm). Cut each square once diagonally to make 32 triangles.

Border 4
From Fabric 17 and cutting along the *length* of the fabric, cut 2 matching lengths 6½in x 84½in (16.5cm x 214.6cm) and 2 matching lengths 6½in x 96½in (16.5cm x 245cm).
Note: You may prefer to cut these after you have pieced the quilt, in case your border measurements differ.

Backing
From Fabric 18 cut a piece 104in x 104in (264cm x 264cm).

Binding
From binding Fabric 16 cut sufficient 2½in (6.4cm) strips diagonally across the fabric, which, when joined, will make a length of about 394in (10m). These bias-cut strips will create an angled stripe pattern.

MAKING THE QUILT
Use a ¼in (6mm) seam allowance throughout and refer to Diagrams 1 to 3 on page 121 and Diagram 4 on page 122 as needed.

Centre Panel To make the centre checkerboard, follow Diagram 1 to lay out the 2½in (6.4cm) squares. The various colours alternate with Fabric 1. Sew the squares into rows and press. Now sew the rows together and press. The panel should be 34½in (87.6cm) square at this stage.
Sew a large Fabric 13 triangle to each side of the checkerboard.

Border 1 Alternate Fabric 15 large blossom triangles (see photo on page 118) with the Fabric 14 triangles. Following Diagram 2, sew 3 Fabric 15

large triangles to 4 of the Fabric 14 triangles, and end with smaller Fabric 15 triangles on each end.
Sew two of the pieced borders to the sides of the quilt. Sew Fabric 14 squares to each end of the remaining two borders and sew these longer borders to the top and bottom of the quilt.

Border 2 Sew the shorter lengths to the sides of the quilt and the longer lengths to the top and bottom of the quilt.

Border 3 Using Fabric 10 and Fabric 13 for each of the 4 borders, alternate 11 pairs of the larger triangles with 12 squares, as shown in Diagram 3. On each end of the border, sew a smaller Fabric 10 triangle.
Make 4 corner blocks using a Fabric 13 square with 4 Fabric 10 triangles sewn to each side, as in Diagram 3.
Sew two pieced borders to each side of the quilt. Sew a corner square to each end of the other two pieced borders and then sew these borders to the top and bottom of the quilt.

Border 4 Sew the matching shorter lengths to the sides of the quilt. Sew the remaining two matching lengths to the top and bottom of the quilt.

FINISHING THE QUILT
Press the quilt top and the piece of backing fabric. Layer the quilt top, batting and backing and baste together (see page 148).
Quilt as desired.
Trim the quilt edges and attach the binding to the quilt (see page 149).

DIAGRAM 1

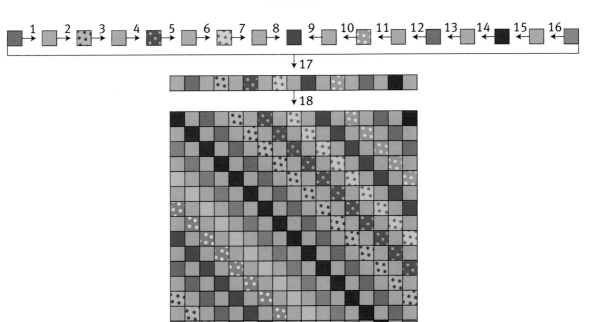

	Fabric 1		Fabric 4		Fabric 7		Fabric 10		Fabric 13		Fabric 16
	Fabric 2		Fabric 5		Fabric 8		Fabric 11		Fabric 14		Fabric 17
	Fabric 3		Fabric 6		Fabric 9		Fabric 12		Fabric 15		

DIAGRAM 2

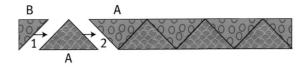

DIAGRAM 3

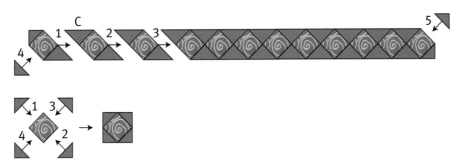

121

DIAGRAM 4

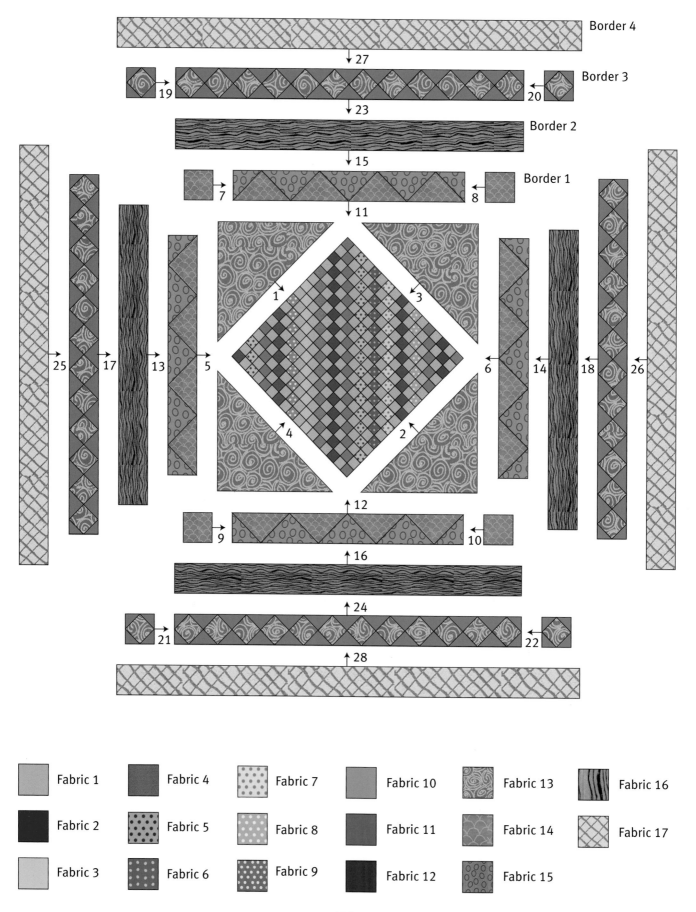

Border 4

Border 3

Border 2

Border 1

Fabric 1
Fabric 2
Fabric 3
Fabric 4
Fabric 5
Fabric 6
Fabric 7
Fabric 8
Fabric 9
Fabric 10
Fabric 11
Fabric 12
Fabric 13
Fabric 14
Fabric 15
Fabric 16
Fabric 17

berry ice cream *

Kaffe Fassett

The simplest form of medallion quilt is one of strips or 'logs' added in 'rounds'. This design starts with a rectangle, which is then surrounded by rounds of different fabrics in varying widths. The strips in each round are added in a clockwise direction, much like a Log Cabin block.

SIZE OF FINISHED QUILT
77½in x 81½in (197cm x 207cm)

FABRICS
Fabrics calculated at minimum width of 40in (102cm) and are cut across the width, unless otherwise stated. Fabrics have been given a number – see Fabric Swatch Diagram for details.

Patchwork Fabrics
ENCHANTED
Fabric 1	Red	¾yd (70cm)
Fabric 2	Dark	¾yd (70cm)

GUINEA FLOWER
Fabric 3	Red	1yd (90cm)

TREFOIL
Fabric 4	Dark	¼yd (25cm)

JUMBLE
Fabric 5	Rust	½yd (45cm)

DIAMOND STRIPE
Fabric 6	Red	1yd (90cm)

ZIG ZAG
Fabric 7	Warm	¾yd (70cm)

LOTUS LEAF
Fabric 8	Wine	1yd (90cm)

PAPERWEIGHT
Fabric 9	Jewel	⅝yd (60cm)

SUCCULENT
Fabric 10	Red	½yd (45cm)

ROW FLOWERS
Fabric 11	Red	1yd (90cm)

Backing and Binding Fabrics
FRUIT MANDALA
Fabric 12	Pink	2½yd (2.3m)

of extra-wide fabric (108in/274cm)
DIAMOND STRIPE
Fabric 6	Red	¾yd (70cm)

Batting
86in x 90in (218.5cm x 229cm)

CUTTING OUT
Centre Panel
From Fabric 1 cut one rectangle 5in x 9in (12.7cm x 22.9cm).

Patchwork Fabrics

Fabric 1
ENCHANTED
Red
GP172RD

Fabric 2
ENCHANTED
Dark
GP172DK

Fabric 3
GUINEA FLOWER
Red
GP59RD

Fabric 4
TREFOIL
Dark
GP167DK

Fabric 5
JUMBLE
Rust
BM53RU

Fabric 6
DIAMOND STRIPE
Red
GP170RD

Fabric 7
ZIG ZAG
Warm
BM43WM

Fabric 8
LOTUS LEAF
Wine
GP29WN

Fabric 9
PAPERWEIGHT
Jewel
GP20JE

Fabric 10
SUCCULENT
Red
PJ91RD

Fabric 11
ROW FLOWERS
Red
GP169RD

Backing and Binding Fabrics

Fabric 12
FRUIT MANDALA
Pink
QBGP003PK

Fabric 6
DIAMOND STRIPE
Red
GP170RD

Strips for each Round
Fabrics 1 to 11 are used in the rounds of the quilt. Cut the strips ('logs') for each round (round 1 to round 20) as given in the Cutting Out Table opposite. All measurements include a ¼in (6mm) seam allowance. The table shows the round number, the fabric used, the log width, the number of width-of-fabric strips needed for each round and the lengths of logs A, B, C and D. The exceptions are Fabric 6, Fabric 7 and Fabric 11, which are cut down the *length* of the fabric (LOF), joining fabric strips as necessary. The final column shows the size the quilt should be after adding each round, including the seam allowance.

Note: Working with narrow strips can be a little tricky. While it is not critical for your quilt to be perfectly sized, it will help if you try to keep your patchwork true after each round is added.

Backing
From Fabric 12 cut a piece 86in x 90in (218.5cm x 229cm).

Binding
From binding Fabric 6 cut sufficient 2½in (6.4cm) strips diagonally across the fabric, which when joined will make a length of at least 330in (838cm). These bias-cut strips will create an angled stripe pattern.

CUTTING OUT TABLE

Note: for the Lavender Ice Cream quilt (see page 128), the number of strips needed are all cut across the *width* of the fabric; for the Berry Ice Cream quilt, asterisk numbers denote fabrics where strips need to be cut down the *length* of fabric (LOF).

Round	Fabric	Log width	# of strips	Log A	Log B	Log C	Log D	Size to raw edge
1	3	1¾in (4.4cm)	1	5in (12.7cm)	10¼in (26cm)	6¼in (16cm)	11½in (29.2cm)	7½in × 11½in (19cm × 29.2cm)
2	2	2in (5.1cm)	2	7½in (19cm)	13in (33cm)	9in (22.9cm)	14½in (36.8cm)	10½in × 14½in (26.7cm × 36.8cm)
3	4	2in (5.1cm)	2	10½in (26.7cm)	16in (40.6cm)	12in (30.5cm)	17½in (44.5cm)	13½in × 17½in (34.3cm × 44.5cm)
4	5	2½in (6.4cm)	2	13½in (34.3cm)	19½in (49.5cm)	15½in (39.4cm)	21½in (54.6cm)	17½in × 21½in (44.5cm × 54.6cm)
5	6	2in (5.1cm)	3 *3 LOF	17½in (44.5cm)	23in (58.4cm)	19in (48.3cm)	24½in (62.2cm)	20½in × 24½in (52cm × 62.2cm)
6	7	1¾in (4.4cm)	3 *4 LOF	20½in (52cm)	25¾in (65.4cm)	21¾in (55.2cm)	27in (68.6cm)	23in × 27in (58.4cm × 68.6cm)
7	8	3in (7.6cm)	3	23in (58.4cm)	29½in (75cm)	25½in (64.8cm)	32in (81.3cm)	28in × 32in (71cm × 81.3cm)
8	9	2in (5.1cm)	4	28in (71cm)	33½in (85cm)	29½in (75cm)	35in (89cm)	31in × 35in (78.7cm × 89cm)
9	5	2in (5.1cm)	4	31in (78.7cm)	36½in (92.7cm)	32½in (82.5cm)	38in (96.5cm)	34in × 38in (86.3cm × 96.5cm)
10	10	3in (7.6cm)	4	34in (86.3cm)	40½in (103cm)	36½in (92.7cm)	43in (109.2cm)	39in × 43in (99cm × 109.2cm)
11	11	2in (5.1cm)	5 *5 LOF	39in (99cm)	44½in (113cm)	40½in (103cm)	46in (116.8cm)	42in × 46in (106.7cm × 116.8cm)
12	3	2½in (6.4cm)	5	42in (106.7cm)	48in (122cm)	44in (111.8cm)	50in (127cm)	46in × 50in (116.8cm × 127cm)
13	6	4in (10.2cm)	6 *8 LOF	46in (116.8cm)	53½in (136cm)	49½in (125.7cm)	57in (144.8cm)	53in × 57in (134.6cm × 144.8cm)
14	9	1½in (3.8cm)	6	53in (134.6cm)	58in (147.3cm)	54in (137.2cm)	59in (149.8cm)	55in × 59in (139.7cm × 149.8cm)
15	11	2½in (6.4cm)	6 *7 LOF	55in (139.7cm)	61in (155cm)	57in (144.8cm)	63in (160cm)	59in × 63in (149.8cm × 160cm)
16	3	2in (5.1cm)	7	59in (149.8cm)	64½in (163.8cm)	60½in (153.7cm)	66in (167.7cm)	62in × 66in (157.5cm × 167.7cm)
17	2	2½in (6.4cm)	7	62in (157.5cm)	68in (172.7cm)	64in (162.5cm)	70in (177.8cm)	66in × 70in (167.7cm × 177.8cm)
18	1	2½in (6.4cm)	7	66in (167.6cm)	72in (183cm)	68in (172.7cm)	74in (188cm)	70in × 74in (177.8cm × 188cm)
19	7	2in (5.1cm)	8 *11 LOF	70in (177.8cm)	75½in (191.8cm)	71½in (181.6cm)	77in (195.6cm)	73in × 77in (185.4cm × 195.6cm)
20	8	3in (7.6cm)	8	73in (185.4cm)	79½in (202cm)	75½in (191.8cm)	82in (208.3cm)	78in × 82in (198cm × 208.3cm)

MAKING THE QUILT

Use a ¼in (6mm) seam allowance throughout. As you make the quilt, try to sew seams in opposite directions as this will help to keep the quilt square.

Take the centre panel and following Diagram 1 sew Round 1 Log A to the bottom of the centre panel and press. Sew Log B to the left-hand side and press. Sew Log C to the top and press and then Log D to the right-hand side and press.

Add Round 2 in the same way, as shown in Diagram 2. In every round the logs are added in the same sequence. Add all 20 rounds of logs as shown in Diagram 3.

DIAGRAM 1

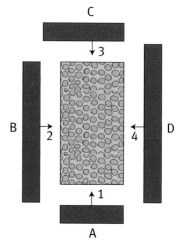

DIAGRAM 2

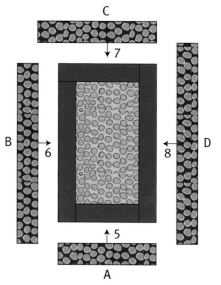

DIAGRAM 3

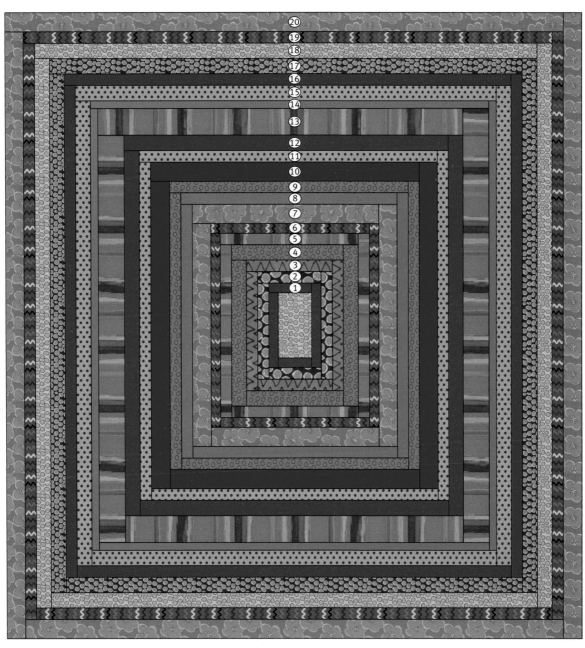

Numbers on Diagram 3 denote the rounds

FINISHING THE QUILT
Press the quilt top and the backing.
Layer the quilt top, batting and backing
and baste together (see page 148).
Quilt as desired.
Trim the quilt edges and attach the
binding (see page 149).

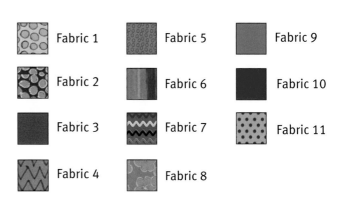

Fabric 1

Fabric 2

Fabric 3

Fabric 4

Fabric 5

Fabric 6

Fabric 7

Fabric 8

Fabric 9

Fabric 10

Fabric 11

lavender ice cream *

Kaffe Fassett

If your tastes run to lavenders and lilacs with a dash of turquoise, then this pretty version of the Berry Ice Cream quilt is for you. It is made in exactly the same way as the quilt on page 123.

SIZE OF FINISHED QUILT
77½in x 81½in (197cm x 207cm)

FABRICS
Fabrics calculated at minimum width of 40in (102cm) and are cut across the width, unless otherwise stated. Fabrics have been given a number – see Fabric Swatch Diagram for details.

Patchwork Fabrics
SUCCULENT
Fabric 1	Grey	¾yd (70cm)

LACY LEAF
Fabric 2	Pastel	¾yd (70cm)

ABORIGINAL DOT
Fabric 3	Lilac	1yd (90cm

ROMAN GLASS
Fabric 4	Pink	¼yd (25cm)

SPOT
Fabric 5	Lavender	½yd (45cm)

ORCHID
Fabric 6	Cool	1yd (90cm)

GOOD VIBRATIONS
Fabric 7	Pink	¾yd (70cm)

BAROQUE FLORAL
Fabric 8	Lavender	1yd (90cm)

MAD PLAID
Fabric 9	Stone	⅝yd (60cm)

GUINEA FLOWER
Fabric 10	Turquoise	½yd (45cm)

MILLEFIORE
Fabric 11	Pink	¾yd (70cm)

Backing and Binding Fabrics
ORCHID
Fabric 6	Cool	5¾yd (5.25m)

GUINEA FLOWER
Fabric 10	Turquoise	¾yd (70cm)

Batting
86in x 90in (218.5cm x 229cm)

Patchwork Fabrics

Fabric 1
SUCCULENT
Grey
PJ91GY

Fabric 2
LACY LEAF
Pastel
PJ93PT

Fabric 3
ABORIGINAL DOT
Lilac
GP71LI

Fabric 4
ROMAN GLASS
Pink
GP01PK

Fabric 5
SPOT
Lavender
GP70LV

Fabric 6
ORCHID
Cool
PJ92CL

Fabric 7
GOOD VIBRATIONS
Pink
BM65PK

Fabric 8
BAROQUE FLORAL
Lavender
PJ90LV

Fabric 9
Mad Plaid
Stone
BM37ST

Fabric 10
GUINEA FLOWER
Turquoise
GP59TQ

Fabric 11
MILLEFIORE
Pink
GP92PK

Backing and Binding Fabrics

Fabric 6
ORCHID
Cool
PJ92CL

Fabric 10
GUINEA FLOWER
Turquoise
GP59TQ

CUTTING OUT
Centre Panel
From Fabric 1 cut one rectangle 5in x 9in (12.7cm x 22.9cm).

Strips for each Round
Fabrics 1 to 11 are used in the rounds of the quilt. Cut the strips ('logs') for each 'round' ('rounds' 1 to 20) as given in the Cutting Out Table on page 125. All measurements include a ¼in (6mm) seam allowance. The table shows the round number, the fabric used, the log width, the number of width-of-fabric strips needed for each round and the lengths of logs A, B, C and D. The final column shows the size the quilt should be after adding each round, including the seam allowance.

Note: Working with narrow strips can be a little tricky. While it is not critical for your quilt to be perfectly sized, it will help if you try to keep your patchwork true after each round is added.

Backing
From backing Fabric 6 cut 2 pieces 40in x 90in (101.6cm x 228.6cm). Cut the remaining yardage into 3 lengths 8in (20.3cm) wide x 25½in (64.8cm) and one length 8in (20.3cm) wide x 15½in (39.4cm).

Binding
From binding Fabric 10 cut 9 strips 2½in (6.4cm) wide across the width of the fabric. Sew together end to end.

MAKING THE QUILT
Refer to the Berry Ice Cream quilt on page 126.

FINISHING THE QUILT
Press the quilt top. Sew the narrow pieces of backing together end to end and trim to 90in (228.6cm). Sew this strip between the larger pieces of backing. Refer to the Berry Ice Cream on page 127 for quilting and finishing.

DIAGRAM 1

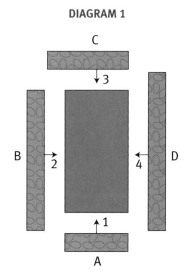

DIAGRAM 2

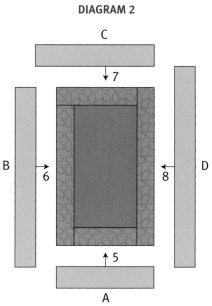

DIAGRAM 3

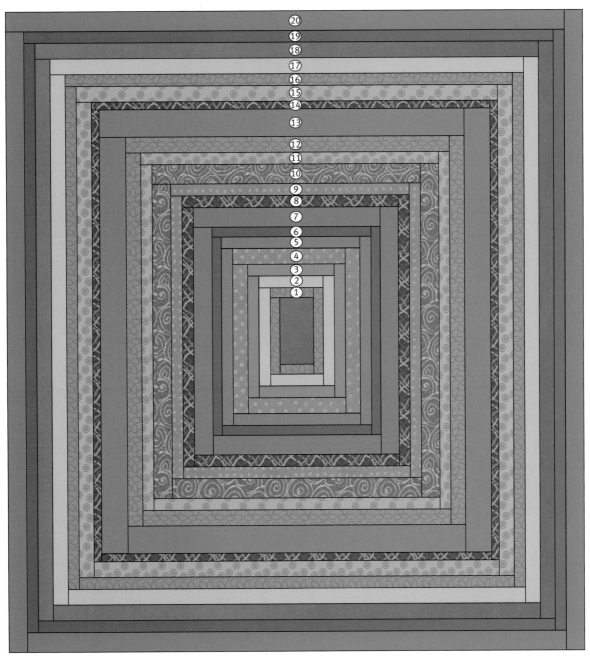

Numbers on Diagram 3 denote the rounds

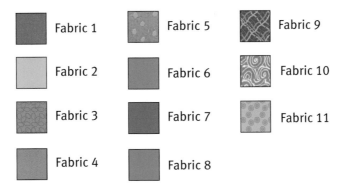

Fabric 1
Fabric 2
Fabric 3
Fabric 4
Fabric 5
Fabric 6
Fabric 7
Fabric 8
Fabric 9
Fabric 10
Fabric 11

chartreuse basket ***

Judy Baldwin

This pretty, but quite complex quilt has some quirky features, such as the freeform appliqué flowers in the central square, the off-centre arrangement of the squares on point in Border 2, the curvy lines and circles in Border 4 and the asymmetrically pieced strips in Border 5. The appliqué for this quilt can be done using fusible web with raw-edge machine appliqué or by using a turned-edge hand appliqué technique. If you choose the fusible web method, fuse the web to the appliqué fabrics before cutting out the shapes. If choosing to appliqué by hand, remember to cut the shapes large enough to turn under a seam allowance.

SIZE OF FINISHED QUILT
70in x 70in (178cm x 178cm)

FABRICS
Fabrics calculated at minimum width of 40in (102cm) and are cut across the width, unless otherwise stated. Fabrics have been given a number – see Fabric Swatch Diagram for details.

Patchwork Fabrics
SPOT
Fabric 1	Pond	2yd (1.8m)
Fabric 2	Bottle	⅛yd (15cm)
Fabric 3	Eggplant	¼yd (25cm)

MILLEFIORE
Fabric 4	Antique	¼yd (25cm)

ABORIGINAL DOT
Fabric 5	Ocean	¼yd (25cm)
Fabric 6	Charcoal	½yd (45cm)

PAPERWEIGHT
Fabric 7	Purple	¾yd (70cm)
Fabric 8	Algae	½yd (45cm)
Fabric 9	Blue	¼yd (25cm)

ZIG ZAG
Fabric 10	Moody	¾yd (70cm)

COLEUS
Fabric 11	Lavender	1½yd (1.4m)

Backing and Binding Fabrics
SUNBURST
Fabric 12	Blue	5yd (4.5m)

ABORIGINAL DOT
Fabric 5	Ocean	¾yd (70cm)

Batting
78in x 78in (198cm x 198cm)

Fusible web
Optional, for flowers and basket handles

TEMPLATES
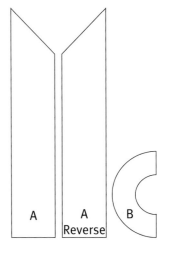

FABRIC SWATCH DIAGRAM

Patchwork Fabrics

Fabric 1
SPOT
Pond
GP70P0

Fabric 2
SPOT
Bottle
GP70BT

Fabric 3
SPOT
Eggplant
GP70EG

Fabric 4
MILLEFIORE
Antique
GP92AN

Fabric 5
ABORIGINAL DOT
Ocean
GP71ON

Fabric 6
ABORIGINAL DOT
Charcoal
GP71CC

Fabric 7
PAPERWEIGHT
Purple
GP20PU

Fabric 8
PAPERWEIGHT
Algae
GP20AL

Fabric 9
PAPERWEIGHT
Blue
GP20BL

Fabric 10
ZIG ZAG
Moody
BM43MO

Fabric 11
COLEUS
Lavender
PJ30LV

Backing and Binding Fabrics

Fabric 12
SUNBURST
Blue
GP162BL

Fabric 5
ABORIGINAL DOT
Ocean
GP71ON

CUTTING OUT

Cut across the width of fabric unless otherwise stated and cut the largest pieces first, if you can.

Centre Panel

Background From Fabric 1 cut one rectangle 10½in x 20in (26.7cm x 50.8cm) and one square 11in (28cm). Cut the square diagonally once, into two triangles. From Fabric 1 and using Template A, cut a strip with an angled end (a seam allowance is included). Cut another strip using Template A Reverse. Note that the direction of the fabric grain has to be horizontal with the length of each strip.

Basket From Fabric 4 cut 12 squares 2½in (6.4cm). Cut each square once diagonally to make 24 triangles (you will use 23).
From Fabric 6 cut 8 squares 2½in (6.4cm). Cut each square once diagonally to make 16 triangles (you will only use 15).
From Fabric 4 use Template B to cut two handles. If using turned-edge appliqué, cut larger to include a seam allowance.

Flowers From Fabric 7 cut 4 free-form flower shapes. On the quilt shown, the finished shapes are approximately 4½in (11.4cm) in diameter.
From Fabric 5 cut 4 free-form flower centres. On the quilt shown, the finished ovals are approximately 1¼in x 1½in (3.2cm x 3.8cm).

Border 1

From Fabric 6 cut 2 strips 1½in x 19½in (3.8cm x 49.5cm) for the sides of the quilt and 2 strips 1½in x 21½in (3.8cm x 54.6cm) for the top and bottom.

Border 2

From Fabric 10 cut 2 strips across the width of the fabric. From these cut 2 strips 4½in x 9½in (11.4cm x 24.1cm) and 2 strips 4½in x 18in (11.4cm x 45.7cm).
From Fabric 10 cut 2 squares 4⅞in (12.4cm). Cut each square diagonally once to make 2 triangles from each square.
From Fabric 10 cut 6 squares 5⅜in (13.7cm). Cut each square diagonally both ways to make 4 triangles from each square.
From Fabric 2 cut 24 squares 2in (5.1cm).
From Fabric 4 cut 24 squares 2in (5.1cm).

Border 3

From Fabric 6 cut 2 strips 1½in x 29½in (3.8cm x 75cm) for the sides of the quilt and 2 strips 1½in x 31½in (3.8cm x 80cm) for the top and bottom.

Border 4

From Fabric 1 cut 4 strips 5¼in x 31½in (13.3cm x 80cm).
From Fabric 11 cut 4 squares 5¼in (13.3cm) for the corner squares.
From Fabric 11 cut 16 circles 1¾in (4.4cm) diameter. If using turned-edge appliqué, cut these larger to include a seam allowance.
From Fabric 8 for the stems, cut 4 strips on the *bias* 1¼in x 40in (3.2cm x 101.6cm) (includes seam allowance). (Join strips to make lengths long enough.)

Border 5

This border is made up of random lengths of 5 different fabrics. Cut 3 strips 2in (5.1cm) wide across the fabric width from Fabric 3, Fabric 5, Fabric 9, Fabric 10 and Fabric 11.

Border 6

From Fabric 1 cut 15 strips 2½in (6.4cm) wide across the width of the fabric. From these, cut 232 squares 2½in (6.4cm).
From Fabric 11 cut 15 strips 2½in (6.4cm) wide across the width of the fabric. From these, cut 232 squares 2½in (6.4cm).

Border 7

From Fabric 7 cut 7 strips 2½in (6.4cm) wide across the width of the fabric. Join as necessary and then cut 2 strips 2½in x 66½in (6.4cm x 169cm) for the sides of the quilt and 2 strips 2½in x 70½in (6.4cm x 179cm) for the top and bottom of the quilt.

Backing

From Fabric 12 cut two pieces each 78in (198cm) long and sew together to make a backing 78in x 78in (198cm x 198cm).

Binding

From binding Fabric 5 cut 8 strips 2½in (6.4cm) wide across the width of the fabric. Sew together end to end.

MAKING THE QUILT

For a brief description of the appliqué methods, see Patchwork Know-how page 147. The quilt assembly is described from the centre outwards, with Diagrams 1, 2, 3 (on page 135) and Diagram 4 (on page 136) to illustrate. For each border, unless otherwise instructed, add the side strips first and then the top and bottom, pressing after every seam. Refer to Diagram 5 (on page 136) and Diagram 6 (on page 137) for the stages of the quilt assembly.

Centre Panel Sew the basket triangles together as in Diagram 1a. Sew a small triangle to the end of piece A and A Reverse (Diagram 1b). Add these to the basket sides and then add the larger triangle to the bottom. Now add the large rectangle to the top and the large triangles to the sides, to complete the centre panel (Diagram 2). Check that the quilt is 19½in (49.5cm) square at this stage. Appliqué the flowers and basket handles into position, using your preferred method. Appliqué the bottom flower so it overlaps the basket a little (Diagram 3).

Border 1 Sew the shorter strips to the sides of the centre panel. Sew the longer strips to the top and bottom.

Border 2 Using the 2in (5.1cm) squares of Fabric 2 and Fabric 4, make 12 four-patch units. For the 2 side borders, follow Diagram 4a and piece together 3 of the four-patch units with 6 small triangles and one large triangle of Fabric 10. For the 9½in (24.1cm) long strip of Fabric 10, trim the lower end at a 45-degree angle, as shown in the diagram, stitch it to the assembled strip and press. Trim the long rectangle if need be so the border measures 21½in (54.6cm) long (Diagram 4b). Make the other side border in the same way and sew into place, easing to fit.
Repeat this process to make the top and bottom borders using the 18in (45.7cm) long strip and this time trim the pieced border to a length of 29½in (75cm). Sew these longer borders into position, easing to fit (Diagram 5).

DIAGRAM 1

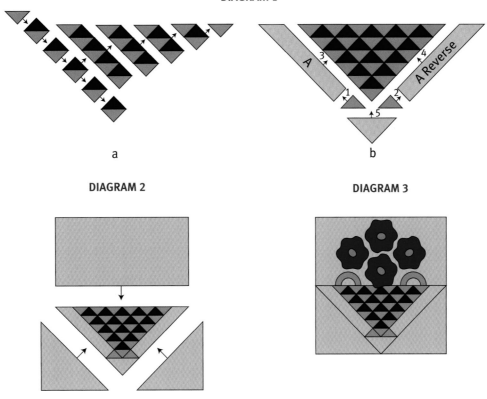

a

b

DIAGRAM 2

DIAGRAM 3

Border 3 Sew the shorter strips to the sides of the quilt. Sew the longer strips to the top and bottom.

Border 4 Sew two shorter Fabric 1 strips to the sides of the quilt. Sew a Fabric 11 corner square to each end of the remaining Fabric 1 strips and then sew these to the top and bottom of the quilt. Prepare the 16 appliqué circles and the bias strip stems using your preferred method. Follow the quilt photograph and Diagram 6 to arrange the bias stems in gently undulating lines along each border strip, with the circles spaced out as shown, and then sew into position.

Border 5 This border has mitred corners. Using the 2in (5.1cm) strips cut random lengths from Fabrics 3, 5, 9, 10 and 11. Mix up the lengths and the fabrics and sew them together end to end to make 12 lengths measuring 52in (132cm). Take 3 lengths and sew them together along their long sides. Repeat with the remaining 9 lengths so you have 4 pieced borders. Sew a border to all four sides of the quilt, stopping ¼in (6mm) from each end. Now mitre the border corners. When sewn, the quilt should measure 50½in (128.3cm) square.

Border 6 Sew the 2½in (6.4cm) squares of Fabric 1 and Fabric 11 into checkerboard-style panels. For the sides of the quilt make the panels 4 x 25 squares and sew into place. For the top and bottom of the quilt make the panels 4 x 33 squares and sew into place.

Border 7 Sew the shorter strips to the sides of the quilt. Sew the longer strips to the top and bottom.

FINISHING THE QUILT
Press the quilt top. Layer the quilt top, batting and backing and baste together (see page 148).
Quilt as desired.
Trim the quilt edges and attach the binding (see page 149).

DIAGRAM 4

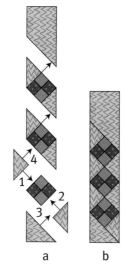

a   b

DIAGRAM 5

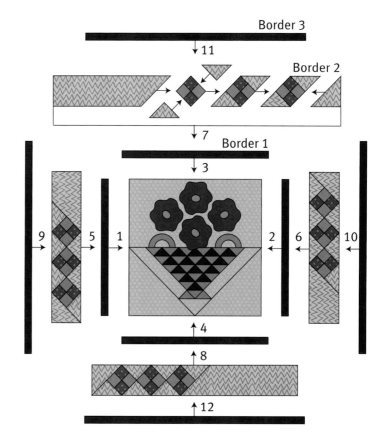

136

DIAGRAM 6

Border 7

Border 6

↓ 27

↓ 23

Border 5

↓ 19

Border 4

↓ 15

25 → 21 → 17 → 13 →

← 14 ← 18 ← 22 ← 26

↑ 16

↑ 20

↑ 24

↑ 28

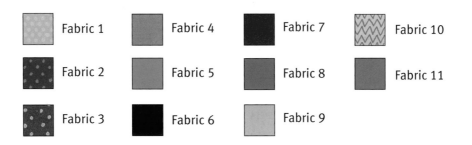

Fabric 1	Fabric 4	Fabric 7	Fabric 10
Fabric 2	Fabric 5	Fabric 8	Fabric 11
Fabric 3	Fabric 6	Fabric 9	

templates

Refer to the individual quilt instructions for the templates needed. Look for the quilt name on the templates, to make sure you are using the correct shapes for the project. Arrows on templates should be lined up with the straight grain of the fabric, which runs either along the selvedge or at 90 degrees to the selvedge. Following marked grain lines is important to avoid bias edges, which can cause distortion.

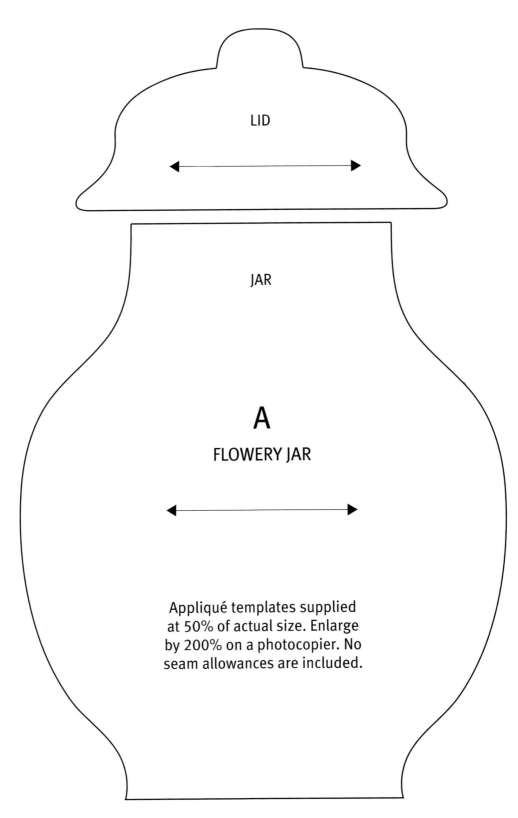

LID

JAR

A

FLOWERY JAR

Appliqué templates supplied at 50% of actual size. Enlarge by 200% on a photocopier. No seam allowances are included.

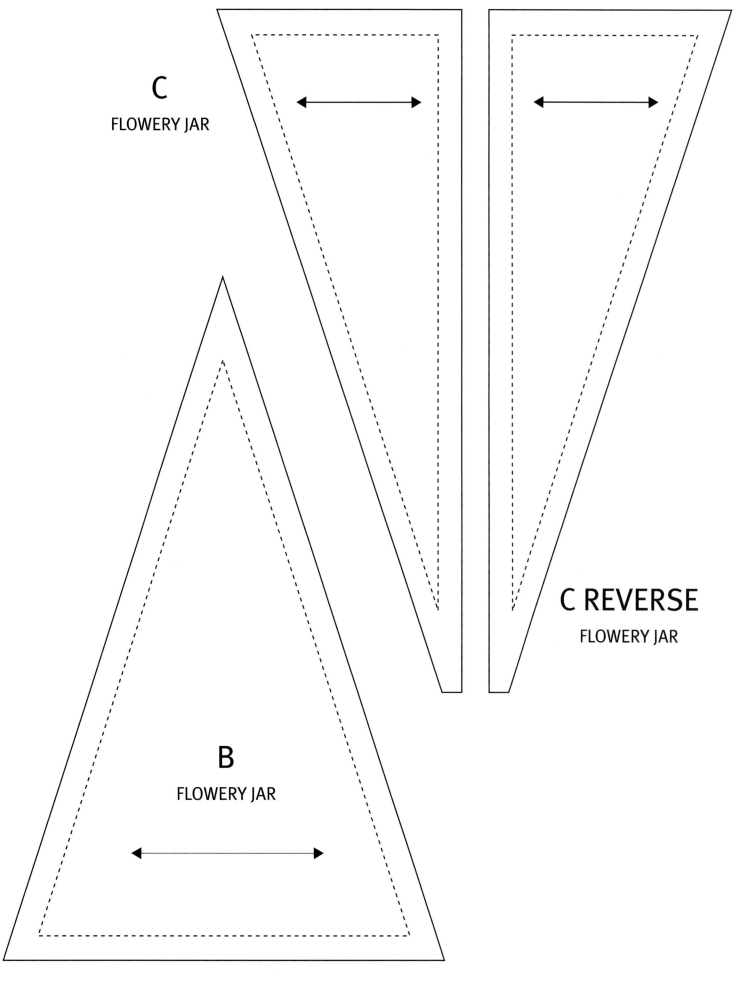

C

FLOWERY JAR

C REVERSE

FLOWERY JAR

B

FLOWERY JAR

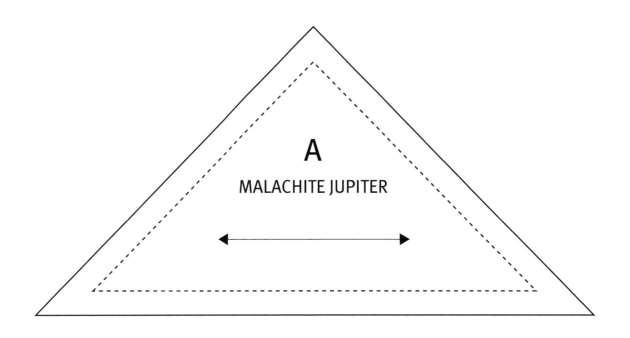

A

MALACHITE JUPITER

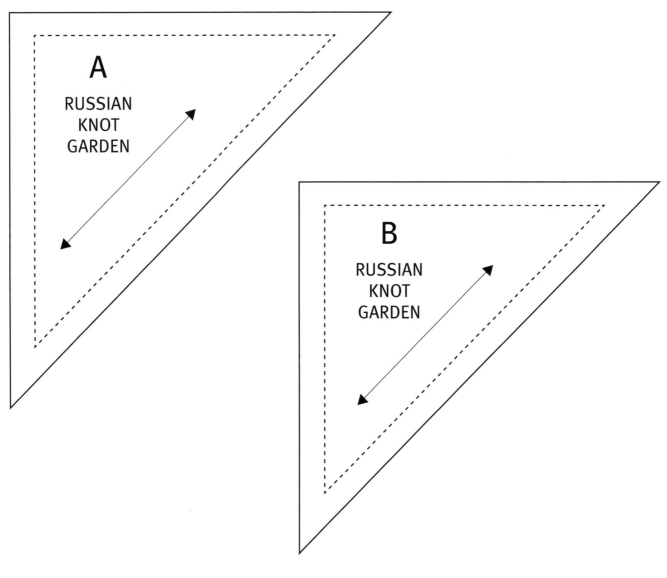

A

RUSSIAN
KNOT
GARDEN

B

RUSSIAN
KNOT
GARDEN

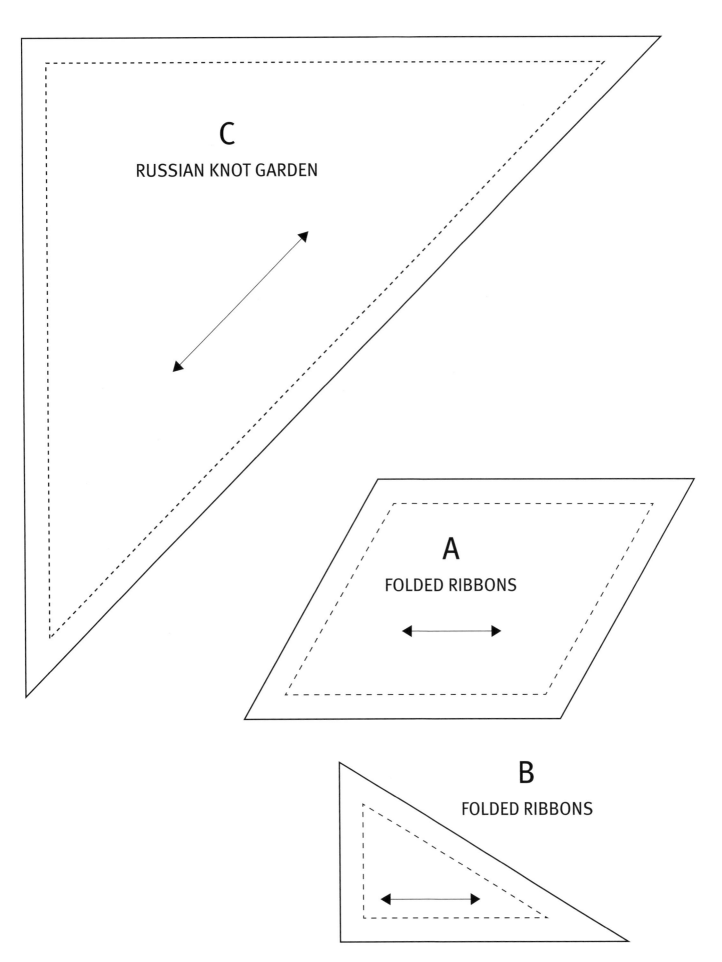

C

RUSSIAN KNOT GARDEN

A

FOLDED RIBBONS

B

FOLDED RIBBONS

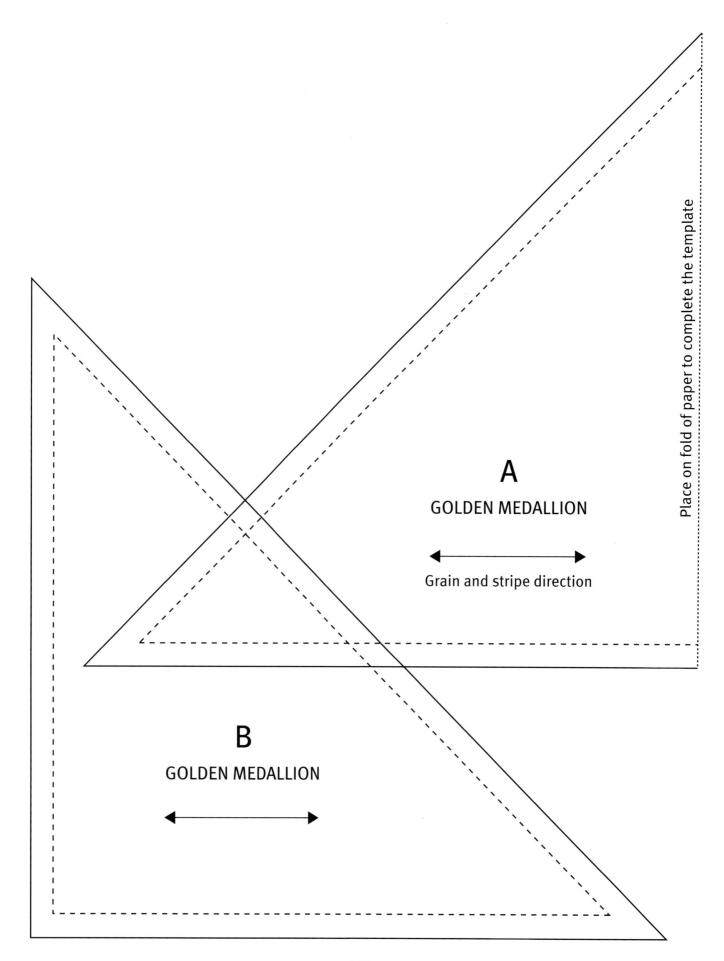

A

GOLDEN MEDALLION

Grain and stripe direction

B

GOLDEN MEDALLION

Place on fold of paper to complete the template

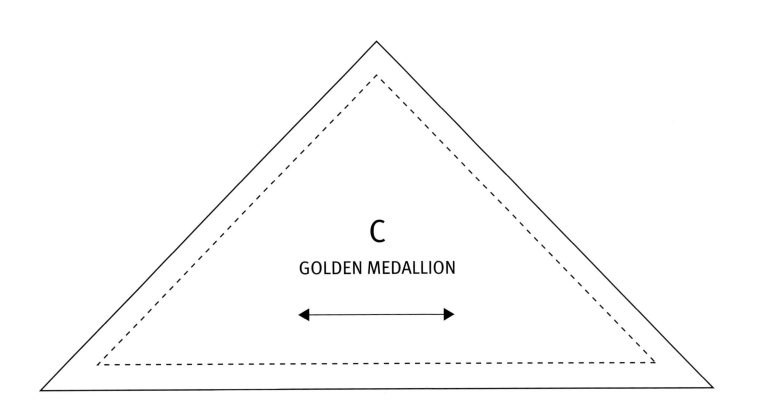

C

GOLDEN MEDALLION

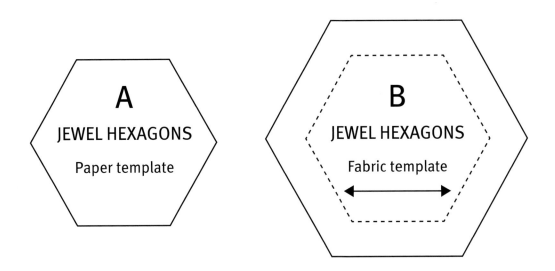

A

JEWEL HEXAGONS

Paper template

B

JEWEL HEXAGONS

Fabric template

143

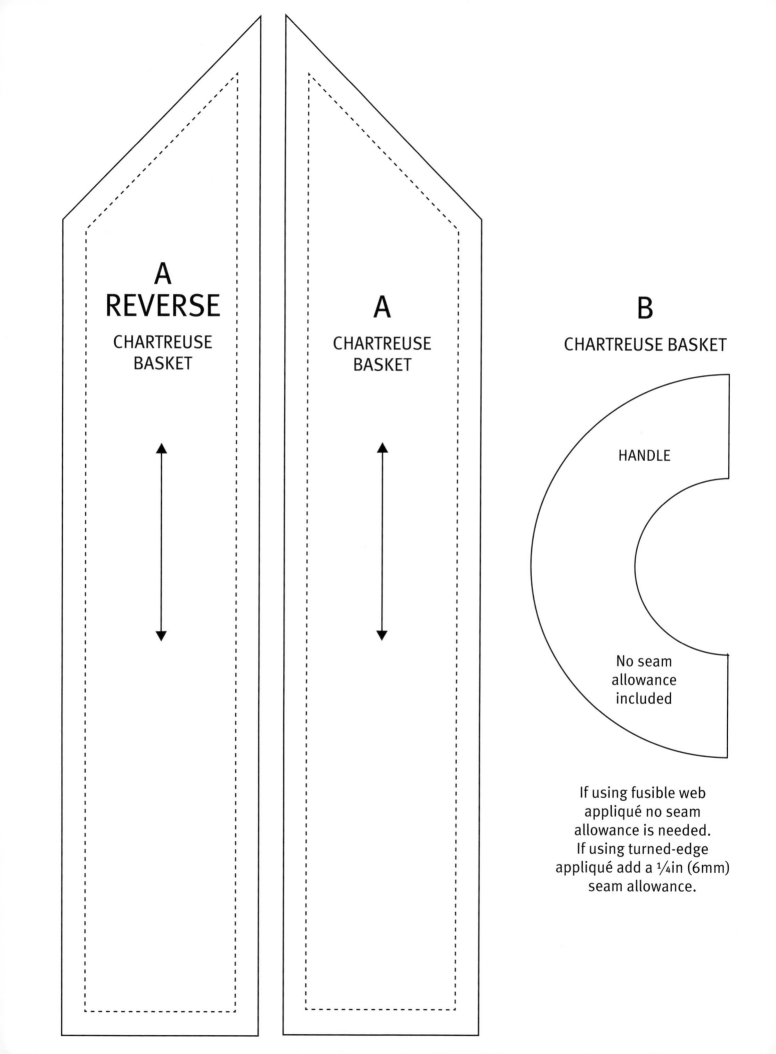

A
REVERSE
CHARTREUSE
BASKET

A
CHARTREUSE
BASKET

B
CHARTREUSE BASKET

HANDLE

No seam
allowance
included

If using fusible web
appliqué no seam
allowance is needed.
If using turned-edge
appliqué add a ¼in (6mm)
seam allowance.

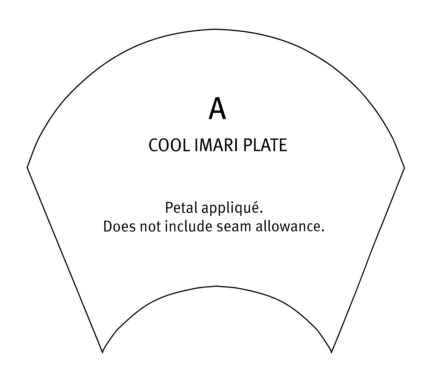

A

COOL IMARI PLATE

Petal appliqué.
Does not include seam allowance.

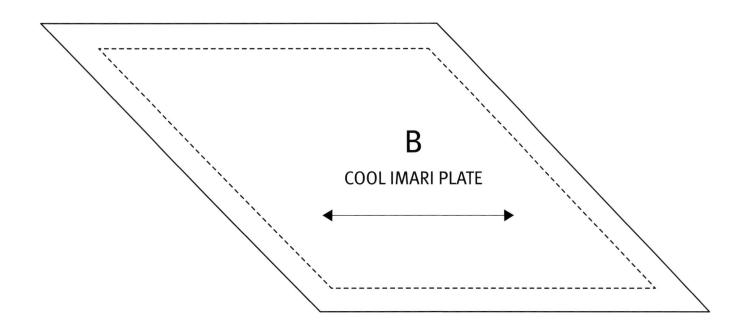

B

COOL IMARI PLATE

patchwork know-how

These instructions are intended for the novice quilt maker, providing the basic information needed to make the projects in this book, along with some useful tips.

EXPERIENCE RATINGS
* Easy, straightforward, suitable for a beginner.
** Suitable for the average patchwork and quilter.
*** For the more experienced patchwork and quilter.

ABOUT THE FABRICS
The fabrics used for the quilts in this book are mainly from Kaffe Fassett Collective:
GP is the code for Kaffe Fassett's designs, PJ for Philip Jacobs' and BM for Brandon Mably's. The other fabrics used are Kaffe Fassett's Sew Artisan. The prefix PWKF is for the prints and the prefix PWBK is for the batiks.

PREPARING THE FABRIC
Prewash all new fabrics before you begin, to ensure that there will be no uneven shrinkage and no bleeding of colours when the finished quilt is laundered. Press the fabric whilst it is still damp to return crispness to it. All fabric requirements in this book are calculated on a 40in (101.5cm) usable fabric width, to allow for shrinkage and selvedge removal.

MAKING TEMPLATES
Transparent template plastic is the best material to use: it is durable and allows you to see the fabric and select certain motifs. You can also use thin stiff cardboard.

Templates for machine piecing
1 Trace off the actual-sized template provided either directly on to template plastic, or tracing paper, and then on to thin cardboard. Use a ruler to help you trace off the straight cutting line, dotted seam line and grain lines.
    Sometimes templates are too large to print complete. Transfer the template onto the fold of a large sheet of paper, cut out and open out for the full template.
2 Cut out the traced off template using a craft knife, a ruler and a self-healing cutting mat.
3 Punch holes in the corners of the template, at each point on the seam line, using a hole punch.

Templates for hand piecing
• Make a template as for machine piecing, but do not trace off the cutting line. Use the dotted seam line as the outer edge of the template.

• This template allows you to draw the seam lines directly on to the fabric. The seam allowances can then be cut by eye around the patch.

CUTTING THE FABRIC
On the individual instructions for each project, you will find a summary of all the patch shapes used.
    Always mark and cut out any border and binding strips first, followed by the largest patch shapes and finally the smallest ones, to make the most efficient use of your fabric. The border and binding strips are best cut using a rotary cutter.

Rotary cutting
Rotary cut strips are usually cut across the fabric from selvedge to selvedge, but some projects may vary, so please read through all the instructions before you start cutting the fabrics.

1 Before beginning to cut, press out any folds or creases in the fabric. If you are cutting a large piece of fabric, you will need to fold it several times to fit the cutting mat. When there is only a single fold, place the fold facing you. If the fabric is too wide to be folded only once, fold it concertina-style until it fits your mat. A small rotary cutter with a sharp blade will cut up to six layers of fabric; a large cutter up to eight layers.

2 To ensure that your cut strips are straight and even, the folds must be placed exactly parallel to the straight edges of the fabric and along a line on the cutting mat.

3 Place a plastic ruler over the raw edge of the fabric, overlapping it about ½in (1.25cm). Make sure that the ruler is at right angles to both the straight edges and the fold to ensure that you cut along the straight grain. Press down on the ruler and wheel the cutter away from you along the edge of the ruler.

4 Open out the fabric to check the edge. Don't worry if it's not perfectly straight – a little wiggle will not show when the quilt is stitched together. Re-fold fabric, then place the ruler over the trimmed edge, aligning the edge with the markings on the ruler that match the correct strip width. Cut strip along the edge of the ruler.

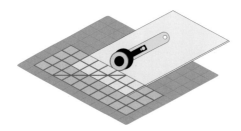

USING TEMPLATES
The most efficient way to cut out templates is by first rotary cutting a strip of fabric to the width stated for your template, and then marking off your templates along the strip, edge to edge at the required angle. This method leaves hardly any waste and gives a random effect to your patches.
    A less efficient method is to fussy cut them, where the templates are cut individually by placing them on particular motifs or stripes, to create special effects. Although this method is more wasteful, it yields very interesting results.

1 Place the template face down, on the wrong side of the fabric, with the grain-line arrow following the straight grain of the fabric, if indicated. Be careful though – check with your individual instructions, as some instructions may ask you to cut patches on varying grains.

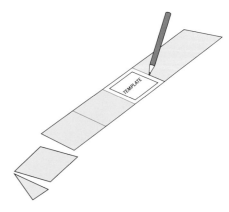

2 Hold the template firmly in place and draw around it with a sharp pencil or crayon, marking in the corner dots or seam lines. To save fabric, position patches close together or even touching. Don't worry if outlines positioned on the straight grain when drawn on striped fabrics do not always match the stripes when cut – this will add a degree of visual excitement to the patchwork!

3 Once you've drawn all the pieces needed, you are ready to cut the fabric, with either a rotary cutter and ruler or a pair of sharp sewing scissors.

BASIC HAND AND MACHINE PIECING
Patches can be stitched together by hand or machine. Machine stitching is quicker, but hand assembly allows you to carry your patches around with you and work on them in every spare moment. The choice is yours. For techniques that are new to you, practise on scrap pieces of fabric until you feel confident.

Machine piecing

Follow the quilt instructions for the order in which to piece the individual patchwork blocks and then assemble the blocks together in rows.

1 Seam lines are not marked on the fabric for simple shapes, so stitch ¼in (6mm) seams using the machine needle plate, a ¼in (6mm) wide machine foot, or tape stuck to the machine as a guide. Pin two patches with right sides together, matching edges.

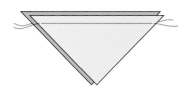

For some shapes, particularly diamonds, you need to match the sewing lines, not the fabric edges. Place 2 diamonds right sides together but offset so that the sewing lines intersect at the correct position. Use pins to secure for sewing.

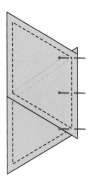

Set your machine at 10–12 stitches per inch (2.5cm) and stitch seams from edge to edge, removing pins as you feed the fabric through the machine.

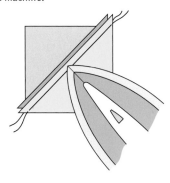

2 Press the seams of each patchwork block to one side before attempting to join it to another block. When joining diamond shaped blocks you will need to offset the blocks in the same way as diamond shaped patches, matching the sewing lines, not the fabric edges.

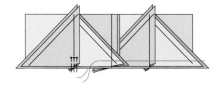

3 When joining rows of blocks, make sure that adjacent seam allowances are pressed in opposite directions to reduce bulk and make matching easier. Pin pieces together directly through the stitch line and to the right and left of the seam. Remove pins as you sew. Continue pressing seams to one side as you work.

Hand piecing

1 Pin two patches with right sides together, so that the marked seam lines are facing outwards.

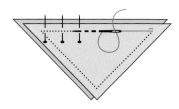

2 Using a single strand of strong thread, secure the corner of a seam line with a couple of back stitches.

3 Sew running stitches along the marked line, working 8–10 stitches per inch (2.5cm) and ending at the opposite seam line corner with a few back stitches. When hand piecing never stitch over the seam allowances.

4 Press the seams to one side, as shown in machine piecing (Step 2).

MACHINE APPLIQUÉ WITH ADHESIVE WEB

To make appliqué very easy you can use adhesive web (which comes attached to a paper backing sheet) to bond the motifs to the background fabric. There are two types of web available: the first keeps the pieces in place while they are stitched, the second permanently attaches the pieces so that no sewing is required. Follow steps 1 and 2 for the non-sew type and steps 1–3 for the type that requires sewing.

1 Trace the reversed appliqué design onto the paper side of the adhesive web, leaving a ¼in (6mm) gap between all the shapes. Roughly cut out the motifs ⅛in (3mm) outside your drawn line.

2 Bond the motifs to the reverse of your chosen fabrics. Cut out on the drawn line with very sharp scissors. Remove the backing paper by scoring the centre of the motif carefully with a scissor point and peeling the paper away from the centre out (to prevent damage to the edges). Place the motifs onto the background, noting any which may be layered. Cover with a clean cloth and bond with a hot iron (check instructions for temperature setting as adhesive web can vary depending on the manufacturer).

3 Using a contrasting or toning coloured thread in your machine, work small close zig zag stitches (or a blanket stitch if your machine has one) around the edge of the

motifs; the majority of the stitching should sit on the appliqué shape. When stitching up to points stop with the machine needle in the down position, lift the foot of your machine, pivot the work, lower the foot and continue to stitch. Make sure all the raw edges are stitched.

HAND APPLIQUÉ

Good preparation is essential for speedy and accurate hand appliqué. The finger-pressing method is suitable for needle-turning application, used for simple shapes like leaves and flowers. Using a card template is the best method for bold simple motifs such as circles.

Finger–pressing method

1 To make your template, transfer the appliqué design using carbon paper on to stiff card, and cut out the template. Trace around the outline of your appliquéd shape on to the right side of your fabric using a well sharpened pencil. Cut out shapes, adding by eye a ¼in (6mm) seam allowance all around.

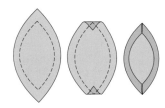

2 Hold the shape right side up and fold under the seam, turning along your drawn line, pinch to form a crease. Dampening the fabric makes this very easy. When using shapes with points such as leaves, turn in the seam allowance at the point first, as shown in the diagram. Then continue all round the shape. If your shapes have sharp curves, you can snip the seam allowance to ease the curve. Take care not to stretch the appliqué shapes as you work.

Straight stems

Place fabric face down and simply press over the ¼in (6mm) seam allowance along each edge. You don't need to finish the ends of stems that are layered under other appliqué shapes. Where the end of the stem is visible, simply tuck under the end and finish neatly.

Needle-turning application

Take the appliqué shape and pin in position. Stroke the seam allowance under with the tip of the needle as far as the creased pencil line, and hold securely in place with your thumb. Using a matching thread, bring the needle up from the back of the block into the edge of the shape and proceed to blind-hem in place. (This stitch allows the motifs to appear to be held on invisibly.) To do this, bring the thread out from below through the folded edge of the motif, never on the top. The stitches must be small, even and close together to prevent the seam allowance from unfolding and from frayed edges appearing. Try to avoid pulling the stitches too tight, as this will cause the motifs to pucker up. Work around the whole shape, stroking under each small section before sewing.

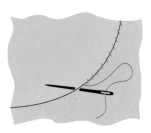

QUILTING
When you have finished piecing your patchwork and added any borders, press it carefully. It is now ready for quilting.

Marking quilting designs and motifs
Many tools are available for marking quilting patterns, check the manufacturer's instructions for use and test on scraps of fabric from your project. Use an acrylic ruler for marking straight lines.

Stencils
Some designs require stencils, these can be made at home, by transferring the designs on to template plastic, or stiff cardboard. The design is then cut away in the form of long dashes, to act as guides for both internal and external lines. These stencils are a quick method for producing an identical set of repeated designs.

BACKING FABRIC
The quilts in this book use two different widths of backing fabric – the standard width of 44in (112cm) and a wider one of 108in (274cm). If you can't find (or don't want to use) the wider fabric then select a standard-width fabric instead and adjust the amount accordingly. For most of the quilts in the book, using a standard-width fabric will probably mean joins in the fabric. The material list for each quilt assumes that an extra 4in of backing fabric is needed all round (8in in total) when making up the quilt sandwich, to allow for long-arm quilting if needed. We have assumed a usable width of 40in (102cm), to allow for selvedge removal and possible shrinkage after washing.

Preparing the backing and batting
• Remove the selvedges and piece together the backing fabric to form a backing at least 4in (10cm) larger all around than the patchwork top.

• Choose a fairly thin batting, preferably pure cotton, to give your quilt a flat appearance. If your batting has been rolled up, unroll it and let it rest before cutting it to the same size as the backing.

• For a large quilt it may be necessary to join two pieces of batting to fit. Lay the pieces of batting on a flat surface so that they overlap by around 8in (20cm). Cut a curved line through both layers.

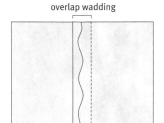

• Carefully peel away the two narrow pieces and discard. Butt the curved cut edges back together. Stitch the two pieces together using a large herringbone stitch.

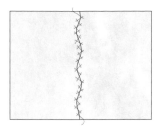

BASTING THE LAYERS TOGETHER
1 On the floor or on a large work surface, lay out the backing with wrong side uppermost. Use weights along the edges to keep it taut.

2 Lay the batting on the backing and smooth it out gently. Next lay the patchwork top, right side up, on top of the batting and smooth gently until there are no wrinkles. Pin at the corners and at the midpoints of each side, close to the edges.

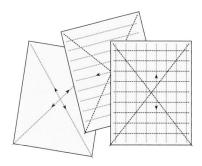

3 Beginning at the centre, baste diagonal lines outwards to the corners, making your stitches about 3in (7.5cm) long. Then, again starting at the centre, baste horizontal and vertical lines out to the edges. Continue basting until you have basted a grid of lines about 4in (10cm) apart over the entire quilt.

4 For speed, when machine quilting, some quilters prefer to baste their quilt sandwich layers together using rust-proof safety pins, spaced at 4in (10cm) intervals over the entire quilt.

HAND QUILTING
This is best done with the quilt mounted on a quilting frame or hoop, but as long as you have basted the quilt well, a frame is not essential. With the quilt top facing upwards, begin at the centre of the quilt and make even running stitches following the design. It is more important to make even stitches on both sides of the quilt than to make small ones. Start and finish your stitching with back stitches and bury the ends of your threads in the batting.

TIED QUILTING
If you prefer you could use tied quilting rather than machine quilting. For tied quilting, use a strong thread that will withstand being pulled through the quilt layers and tied in a knot. You can tie with the knot on the front of the quilt or the back, as preferred. Leaving tufts of thread gives an attractive, rustic look.

Thread a needle with a suitable thread, using the number of strands noted in the project. Put the needle and thread through from the front of the work, leaving a long tail. Go through to the back of the quilt, make a small stitch and then come back through to the front. Tie the threads together using a reef knot and trim the thread ends to the desired length. For extra security, you could tie a double knot or add a spot of fabric glue on the knot.

MACHINE QUILTING

• For a flat looking quilt, always use a walking foot on your machine for stitching straight lines, and a darning foot for free-motion quilting.

• It is best to start your quilting at the centre of the quilt and work out towards the borders, doing the straight quilting lines first (stitch-in-the-ditch) followed by the free-motion quilting.

• When free-motion quilting stitch in a loose meandering style as shown in the diagrams. Do not stitch too closely as this will make the quilt feel stiff when finished. If you wish you can include floral themes or follow shapes on the printed fabrics for added interest.

• Make it easier for yourself by handling the quilt properly. Roll up the excess quilt neatly to fit under your sewing machine arm, and use a table or chair to help support the weight of the quilt that hangs down the other side.

FINISHING

Preparing to bind the edges

Once you have quilted or tied your quilt sandwich together, remove all the basting stitches. Then, baste around the outer edge of the quilt ¼in (6mm) from the edge of the top patchwork layer. Trim the back and batting to the edge of the patchwork and straighten the edge of the patchwork if necessary.

Making the binding

1 Cut bias or straight grain strips the width required for your binding, making sure the grain-line is running the correct way on your straight grain strips. Cut enough strips until you have the required length to go around the edge of your quilt.

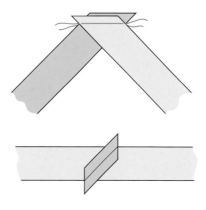

2 To join strips together, the two ends that are to be joined must be cut at a 45 degree angle, as above. Stitch right sides together, trim turnings and press seam open.

Binding the edges

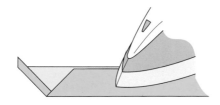

1 Cut the starting end of binding strip at a 45 degree angle, fold a ¼in (6mm) turning to wrong side along cut edge and press in place. With wrong sides together, fold strip in half lengthways, keeping raw edges level, and press.

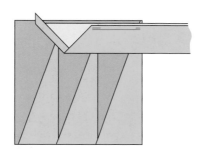

2 Starting at the centre of one of the long edges, place the doubled binding on to the right side of the quilt keeping raw edges level. Stitch the binding in place starting ¼in (6mm) in from the diagonal folded edge. Reverse stitch to secure, and work ¼in (6mm) in from edge of the quilt towards first corner of quilt. Stop ¼in (6mm) in from corner and work a few reverse stitches.

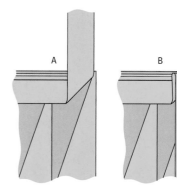

3 Fold the loose end of the binding up, making a 45 degree angle (see A). Keeping the diagonal fold in place, fold the binding back down, aligning the raw edges with the next side of the quilt. Starting at the point where the last stitch ended, stitch down the next side (see B).

4 Continue to stitch the binding in place around all the quilt edges in this way, tucking the finishing end of the binding inside the diagonal starting section.

5 Turn the folded edge of the binding on to the back of the quilt. Hand stitch the folded edge in place just covering binding machine stitches, and folding a mitre at each corner

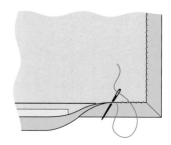

glossary of terms

Adhesive or fusible web This comes attached to a paper-backed sheet and is used to bond appliqué motifs to a background fabric. There are 2 types of web available, the first keeps the pieces in place whilst they are stitched, the second permanently attaches the pieces so that no sewing is required.

Appliqué The technique of stitching fabric shapes on to a background to create a design. It can be applied either by hand or machine with a decorative embroidery stitch, such as buttonhole, or satin stitch.

Backing The bottom layer of a quilt sandwich. It is made of fabric pieced to the size of the quilt top with the addition of about 4in (10.25cm) all around to allow for quilting take-up.

Basting or tacking This is a means of holding two fabric layers or the layers of a quilt sandwich together temporarily with large hand stitches or pins.

Batting or wadding This is the middle layer, or padding in a quilt. It can be made of cotton, wool, silk or synthetic fibres.

Bias The diagonal grain of a fabric. This is the direction which has the most give or stretch, making it ideal for bindings, especially on curved edges.

Binding A narrow strip of fabric used to finish off the edges of quilts or projects; it can be cut on the straight grain of a fabric or on the bias.

Block A single design unit that when stitched together with other blocks create the quilt top. It is most often a square, hexagon, or rectangle, but it can be any shape. It can be pieced or plain.

Border A frame of fabric stitched to the outer edges of the quilt top. Borders can be narrow or wide, pieced or plain. As well as making the quilt larger, they unify the overall design and draw attention to the central area.

Chalk pencils Available in various colours, they are used for marking lines or spots on fabric.

Cutting mat Designed for use with a rotary cutter, it is made from a special self-healing material that keeps your cutting blade sharp. Cutting mats come in various sizes and are usually marked with a grid to help you line up the edges of fabric and cut out larger pieces.

Design wall Used for laying out fabric patches before sewing. A large wall or folding board covered with flannel fabric or cotton batting in a neutral shade (dull beige or grey work well) will hold fabric in place so that an overall view can be taken of the placement.

Free-motion quilting Curved wavy quilting lines stitched in a random manner. Stitching diagrams are often given for you to follow as a loose guide.

Fussy cutting This is when a template is placed on a particular motif, or stripe, to obtain interesting effects. This method is not as efficient as strip cutting, but yields very interesting results.

Grain The direction in which the threads run in a woven fabric. In a vertical direction it is called the lengthwise grain, which has very little stretch. The horizontal direction, or crosswise grain is slightly stretchy, but diagonally the fabric has a lot of stretch. This grain is called the bias. Wherever possible the grain of a fabric should run in the same direction on a quilt block and borders.

Grain lines These are arrows printed on templates which should be aligned with the fabric grain.

Inset seams or setting-in A patchwork technique whereby one patch (or block) is stitched into a V-shape formed by the joining of two other patches (or blocks).

Patch A small shaped piece of fabric used in the making of a patchwork pattern.

Patchwork The technique of stitching small pieces of fabric (patches) together to create a larger piece of fabric, usually forming a design.

Pieced quilt A quilt composed of patches.

Quilting Traditionally done by hand with running stitches, but for speed modern quilts are often stitched by machine. The stitches are sewn through the top, wadding and backing to hold the three layers together. Quilting stitches are usually worked in some form of design, but they can be random.

Quilting hoop Consists of two wooden circular or oval rings with a screw adjuster on the outer ring. It stabilises the quilt layers, helping to create an even tension.

Reducing glass Used for viewing the complete composition of a quilt at a glance. It works like a magnifier in reverse. A useful tool for checking fabric placement before piecing a quilt.

Rotary cutter A sharp circular blade attached to a handle for quick, accurate cutting. It is a device that can be used to cut several layers of fabric at one time. It must be used in conjunction with a self-healing cutting mat and a thick plastic ruler.

Rotary ruler A thick, clear plastic ruler marked with lines in imperial or metric measurements. Sometimes they also have diagonal lines indicating 45 and 60 degree angles. A rotary ruler is used as a guide when cutting out fabric pieces using a rotary cutter.

Sashing A piece or pieced sections of fabric interspaced between blocks.

Sashing posts When blocks have sashing between them the corner squares are known as sashing posts.

Selvedges Also known as selvages, these are the firmly woven edges down each side of a fabric length. Selvedges should be trimmed off before cutting out your fabric, as they are more liable to shrink when the fabric is washed.

Stitch-in-the-ditch or Ditch quilting Also known as quilting-in-the-ditch. The quilting stitches are worked along the actual seam lines, to give a pieced quilt texture.

Template A pattern piece used as a guide for marking and cutting out fabric patches, or marking a quilting, or appliqué design. Usually made from plastic or strong card that can be reused many times. Templates for cutting fabric usually have marked grain lines which should be aligned with the fabric grain.

Threads One hundred percent cotton or cotton-covered polyester is best for hand and machine piecing. Choose a colour that matches your fabric. When sewing different colours and patterns together, choose a medium to light neutral colour, such as grey or ecru. Specialist quilting threads are available for hand and machine quilting.

Walking foot or Quilting foot This is a sewing machine foot with dual feed control. It is very helpful when quilting, as the fabric layers are fed evenly from the top and below, reducing the risk of slippage and puckering.

Yo-Yos A circle of fabric double the size of the finished puff is gathered up into a rosette shape.

Y-seams See Inset seams.

ACKNOWLEDGMENTS

First and foremost, thanks to Brandon Mably for organizing the making of the quilts, and his helpful insights, as well as the many details of getting these books produced.

Thanks to Liza Prior Lucy and Janet Haigh and their respective teams of quilt makers* in the UK and the USA.

For our most glorious location at the National Trust's Hidcote Manor Gardens, thanks to Sarah Malleson, Head Gardener at Hidcote, Michelle Joyce, Visitor Experience Manager, and to Sarah Davis, Harriet Groves and Rosanne Futers.

Thanks also to Lin Clements for her technical expertise, to our PA, Bundle, for her organizational skills, to Anne Wilson for her layouts and attention to detail, and also a big thank you to Debbie Patterson for her insightful eye.

Lastly, special thanks to Carolyn Mandarano of Taunton who, aided and abetted by Susan Berry, our publishing consultant, ensured that this, the 21st in our much-loved series, found a new publishing home.

* Dark Gameboard (Julie Harvey)
  Flowery Jar (Ilaria Padovani)
  Malachite Jupiter (Julie Harvey)
  Russian Knot Garden (Julie Harvey)
  Golden Medallion (Liza Prior Lucy)
  Berry Ice Cream (Corienne Kramer)
  Cool Imari Plate (Corienne Kramer)
  Autumn Chintz (Julie Harvey)
  Jewel Hexagons (Liza Prior Lucy)
  Graphite Medallion (Judy Baldwin)
  Folded Ribbons (Liza Prior Lucy)
  Pink Squares (Ilaria Padovani)
  Glamping Medallion (Ilaria Padovani)
  Sunny Zig Zag (Julie Harvey)
  Blue Square Dance (Julie Harvey)
  Sunny Beyond the Border (Ilaria Padovani)
  Lavender Ice Cream (Bobbi Penniman)
  Chartreuse Basket (Judy Baldwin)
  Autumn Checkerboard (Liza Prior Lucy)

OTHER TAUNTON TITLES AVAILABLE

Kaffe Fassett's Quilt Romance
Kaffe Fassett's Quilts en Provence
Kaffe Fassett's Quilts in Sweden
Kaffe Quilts Again
Kaffe Fassett's Quilt Grandeur

Kaffe Fassett's Quilts in Morocco
Kaffe Fassett's Heritage Quilts
Kaffe Fassett's Quilts in Italy
Kaffe Fassett's Quilts in Ireland
Kaffe Fassett's Quilts in America

The fabric collection can be viewed online at
www.freespiritfabrics.com

The Taunton Press
Inspiration for hands-on living®

The Taunton Press, Inc., 63 South Main Street,
Newtown, CT 06470
Tel: 800-888-8286 • Email: tp@taunton.com
www.tauntonstore.com

KAFFE
FASSETT

—————— for ——————

Free Spirit

Free Spirit Fabrics
Carmel Park II
11121 Carmel Commons Blvd.
Charlotte, NC 28226

distributors and stockists

AUSTRALIA
XLN Fabrics
2/21 Binney Rd
Kings Park
NSW 3283
www.xln.com.au
email: allanmurphy@xln.com.au

CHINA (inc HONG KONG/MACAO)
Wan Mei Diy China
1458 GuMei Road, Room 502-14,
Shanghai 201102
China
email: 12178550@qq.com

DENMARK
Industrial Textiles A/S
Engholm Parkvej 1
Alleroed 3450
email: maria@indutex.dk
www.indutex.dk

EUROPE (SEE ALSO UK/EUROPE)

HONG KONG
Wan Mei Diy China
1458 GuMei Road, Room 502-14,
Shanghai 201102
China
email: 12178550@qq.com

JAPAN
Kiyohara & Co Ltd
4-5-2 Minamikyuhoji-machi Chuo-ku
Osaka 541-8506
www.kiyohara.co.jp

Yamachu-Mengyo Co Ltd
1-10-8 Edobori
Nishi-Ku,
Osaka 550-0002
www.yamachu-mengyo.co.jp

KOREA
Elgatex
103 Park Palace 95,
Naesoo-Dong Jongro-gu,
Seoul, Korea 110901
email: kennyel@unitel.co.kr

June Crafts
5022 B-BLD Dong Dea Mun Chain,
28903 Jongro 6-GA,
Jong Ro Gu,
Seoul, Korea
email: ityrhee@yahoo.com

MACAO
Wan Mei Diy China
1458 GuMei Road, Room 502-14,
Shanghai 201102
China
email: 12178550@qq.com

NEW ZEALAND
Fabco Ltd
43 Lee Martin Road
Hamilton 3283
New Zealand
www.fabco.co.nz
email: melanie@fabco.co.nz

SINGAPORE
Sing Mui Heng
315 Outram
#13-03 Tan Boon Liat Building
Singapore
email: mkt@singmuiheng.com

SOUTH AFRICA
Arthur Bales Pty Ltd
62 4th Avenue
Johannesburg 2103
www.arthurbales.co.za
email: nicci@arthurbales.co.za

SPAIN
Jose Rosas Taberner SA
Ave Mare de Deu de Montserrat 45
P I La Fonstanta
St Joan Despi Barcelona 8970
www.castelltort.com

TAIWAN
Long Teh Trading Co Ltd
No. 71 Hebei W. St
Tai Chung City 40669
Taiwan
email: Longteh.quilt@gmail.com

UK/EUROPE
Rhinetex BV
Maagdenburgstraat 24
ZC Deventer 7421
Netherlands
www.rhinetex.com
email: info@rhinetex.com